# Basic Structure Modeling
## for Model Railroaders

Jeff Wilson

KALMBACH BOOKS

Published by Kalmbach Publishing Co., 21027 Crossroads Circle, Waukesha, WI 53187

15 14 13 12 11    3 4 5 6 7

Manufactured in the United States of America

Visit our website at http://www.Kalmbach.com/Books
Secure online ordering available

Publisher's Cataloging-In-Publication Data

Wilson, Jeff, 1964-
    Basic structure modeling for model railroaders / Jeff Wilson.

    p. : ill. ;  cm.

    ISBN 10: 0-89024-446-4
    ISBN 13: 978-0-89024-446-3

1. Railroads—Models—Design and construction—Handbooks, manuals, etc.
2. Railroads—Models—Finishing—Handbooks, manuals, etc.  I. Title.

TF197 .W55 2005
625.19

Managing Art Director: Mike Soliday
Book Design: Sabine Beaupré

# Contents

**About the Author/Acknowledgments**          **4**

**Introduction**          **5**

Chapter One: **Plastic Kits**          **7**

Chapter Two: **Wood Kits**          **21**

Chapter Three: **Scratchbuilding**          **27**

Chapter Four: **Structure Roofs**          **35**

Chapter Five: **Painting**          **49**

Chapter Six: **Detailing**          **62**

Chapter Seven: **Signs**          **71**

Inspiration: **Photo Gallery**          **82**

**List of Manufacturers**          **86**

## About the Author

*Basic Structure Modeling* is Jeff Wilson's fourteenth book on railroads and model railroading. Jeff has been interested in railroads since childhood and has been building model railroads since his first O-27 layout when he was eight. He is currently modeling the circa-1964 Chicago, Burlington & Quincy in HO scale, and has just started building a new layout (thanks to a move to a new house). He enjoys many facets of the hobby, especially building structures and detailing locomotives. He also enjoys photographing both real and model railroads.

A graduate of St. Cloud (Minnesota) State University, Jeff worked as a sports writer and magazine editor before spending 10 years as an associate editor at *Model Railroader* magazine. He currently works as a free-lance writer, editor, and photographer, contributing articles to *MR* and other magazines. He also writes a model railroading column for *Model Retailer* magazine and is a correspondent for *Trains* magazine.

An avid baseball fan, Jeff spends considerable time in the summer working as a scoreboard operator for the Milwaukee Brewers and playing baseball in local leagues. He also enjoys watching sports and playing volleyball and golf. Other interests include reading, crossword puzzles, and World War II history. He lives in southeast Wisconsin with his wife Sonja and son Mark.

## Acknowledgements

I would like to thank the many people and companies who helped me by providing photos, products, models, and information: Thanks to Dave Proell (JL Innovative Design), Sermeng Tay-Konkol (Wm. K. Walthers), Melanie Buellesbach, Keith Kohlmann, Bob Gallegos, Jim Hediger, Brian Lenzen, Seth Puffer, and George Sebastian-Coleman. Thanks also to American Model Builders, Atlas, Blair Line, Coffman Engineering, Design Preservation Models, Microscale, and Woodland Scenics.

— *Jeff Wilson, February 2005*

A Chicago, Burlington & Quincy freight train ca. 1964 rolls past the Portage, Illinois, tower on the author's old HO layout. This layout has since been torn down, but the structure and trains are being incorporated in a new project.

Chicago Great Western trains also used the trackage at Portage. Here a CGW freight rolls westbound while one of the Burlington's eastbound Zephyrs approaches.

With a few details and signs, you can turn ordinary buildings into impressive street scenes that capture the look of real-life cities and towns.

# Introduction

Structures are among the most important scenic elements on a model railroad. Their design helps place the locale and era of a layout, letting visitors (including those "visiting" via photographs) relate to a scene more vividly.

Since choosing structures is an important part of layout design, you must ask yourself several questions at the outset. First, what are your modeling skills, how much time do you have, how much do you like building structures, and what types of structure kits are you comfortable building? Do you want to stick to built-up models and simple injection-molded styrene kits, or do you want to try craftsman-style kits? Are you modeling a real railroad with unique or special buildings that you'll want to scratchbuild?

## Structure kits

Model structures fall into several categories. Pre-assembled buildings have become more widely available in recent years. An advantage is that the built-up structures being offered are generally of good quality and much more realistic than the toylike Plasticville line of the past. Some disadvantages are that modifying assembled structures is difficult and painting them can be a challenge.

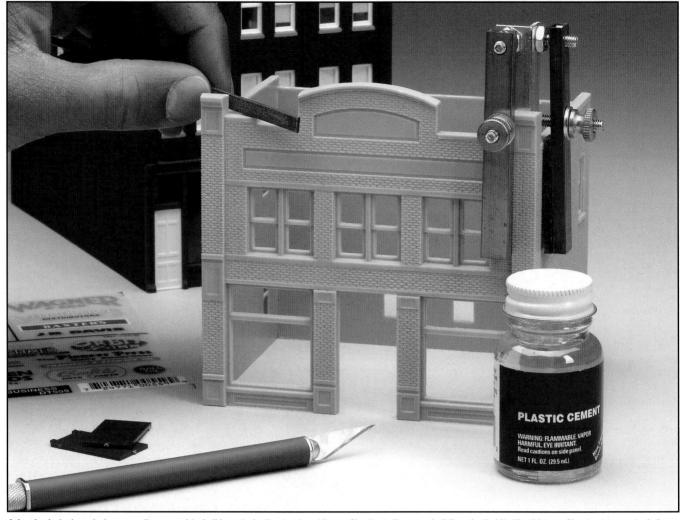

A few basic tools and glues are all you need to build most plastic structure kits, such as this HO scale Design Preservation Models brick storefront structure. Chapter 1 discusses building plastic kits like this one. Chapter 5 covers techniques for painting and finishing model structures.

The next category, the plastic structure kit, represents for many modelers their first attempt at model building. Plastic kits range from easy-to-assemble box-like buildings to complex factory and industrial buildings. Although plastic kits were once regarded as low-quality stand-ins for scratchbuilt or craftsman kits, many modern plastic kits have good detail and are very realistic.

Wood kits fall into a couple of categories. Laser-cut kits have most parts cut to size, and many use peel-and-stick construction for roofing materials and even fine details like window frames. Craftsman-style kits generally require much more cutting and fitting of parts.

## Scratchbuilding

There's also the art of scratchbuilding. Although the thought of building a structure from raw materials intimidates many modelers, it shouldn't, as scratchbuilding a simple structure can be as easy as putting together an intermediate-level kit. In fact, once you've built a few kits, you're probably ready to tackle a simple scratchbuilding project.

Scratchbuilding structures can be loads of fun and is often the only way to duplicate specific buildings found in real life. We'll take a look at the tremendous variety of components available for scratchbuilding, including brick and wall materials, window frames, and other detail parts.

## Structure improvements

Regardless of the type of kits you build or the era or railroad you model, you can do many things to improve the realism and appearance of structures.

Painting is one of the most basic improvements you can do, as you'll find that even kits labeled "molded in realistic colors" really aren't. A coat of paint is also an easy way to make your model different from all the others out there built from the same kit.

We'll look at many ways of bringing structures to life by adding details, from window treatments and interior detail to exterior items such as roof vents, air conditioners, and loading platforms.

Signs are everywhere in real life, and they should decorate model structures as well. Signs bearing familiar logos and names from national and local companies are useful in marking a model railroad's time and place, and can add a great deal of personality.

Turn the page and we'll begin by looking at the basics of assembling plastic and wood structure kits.

**ONE**

# Plastic kits

In the early days of the hobby, the word "plastic" had a stigma, as many modelers scorned plastic structure kits as unrealistic stand-ins for wood craftsman or scratchbuilt structures. That is no longer the case because many plastic structures—even simple ones—have excellent detail and, with some paint and a few extra details, can be showpieces on any model railroad.

Building a simple plastic kit is a good way to get into structure modeling. Some plastic kits are easy to assemble, while others are complex and require time and care to put together. Regardless of the type you choose, mastering a few basic assembly techniques will help you build a realistic structure.

Many characteristics make plastic ideal for structure models: It's moisture-proof, thus resistant to warping from humidity (or wet paint). It's also readily glued by solvents that, when used properly, will melt the bonded surfaces together to make a joint as strong as the plastic itself. Plastic also takes paint well, making it suitable for a variety of finishing and weathering techniques that result in impressively realistic effects (see Chapter 5 for details on painting).

Through the wonders of injection molding, plastic structures come with a variety of realistic relief textures, including brick and concrete block, clapboard and other wood surfaces, textured roofs, and highly ornate window frames, cornices, and details.

Excellent HO and N scale plastic kits are available from several companies, including Atlas, City Classics, Design Preservation Models, Great West Models, Pikestuff, Rix, and Walthers.

Keep a few important things in mind. For starters, be careful gluing joints, especially corners. A poorly aligned corner will throw off the squareness of the whole building, making it difficult or impossible to get other joints aligned properly.

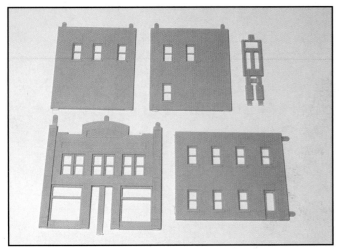

**1** This HO scale building from Design Preservation Models (no. 116, Carr's Parts) is an example of a simple–but well-detailed–structure kit, with all details molded in place. The company makes many similar structures in HO and N scales.

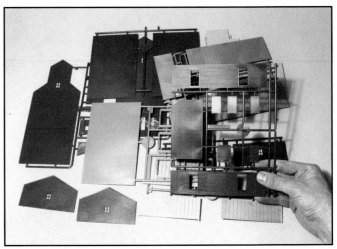

**2** This HO Walthers grain elevator (no. 933-3036) is a bit more complex, with several mini-structure subassemblies and many more parts than the DPM kit.

**3** Make sure the mating edges of butt-jointed walls are square. This True Sander, made by NorthWest Short Line, makes squaring up edges a snap.

**4** Make sure the mating edges of butt-jointed walls are square. The wall at right has been sanded and squared up; the wall at left has not.

Use the proper tools for the task. Assembling plastic kits requires a few special tools and adhesives, described in the sidebars on pages 18 and 19.

Although labels on many kit boxes proudly proclaim that "parts are molded in appropriate colors" and "no painting is necessary," don't believe it. I highly recommend painting all plastic kits, as raw plastic (regardless of color) tends to look like . . . plastic.

## Starting assembly

The first step with any kit is to pull out all of the parts and see what you're working with. Kits can be as simple as four walls and a roof, as with the Design Preservation Models storefront structure in fig. 1, or a complex combination of main structure, auxiliary buildings, details, and window and door frames like the Walthers grain elevator in fig. 2.

Read through the instructions and familiarize yourself with the parts. It's usually best to put things together in subassemblies, which will make later painting and window installation much easier. The usual order for assembly is to put walls together, followed by window and door frames, then roofs, and finally clear window glazing and details.

## Preparation

Probably the most important part of building a kit is making sure corner joints between walls are strong and square. Tight-fitting joints disappear, giving the appearance of a solid structure. Improperly fitting joints with gaps will make even the nicest structure look toylike, and poorly aligned wall joints will make succeeding parts (such as the roof) fit awkwardly as well.

Different kit manufacturers use different wall-joint designs, each of which requires a different assembly technique. Let's start with the Design Preservation Models kit from fig. 1. Like many others, it uses flat molds, so the walls are simply butted against each other. Joints like this require care to get a tight fit.

Make sure the wall edge with the mating surface has a clean 90-degree edge. The wall edges on flat-molded

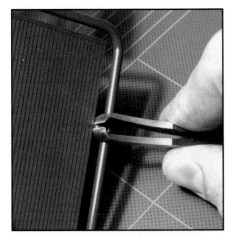

**5** Sprue cutters do an excellent job of neatly separating parts from their sprues. If this is done properly, little cleaning up is necessary.

**6** A chisel-tip hobby knife also works well for cutting sprue. Take care not to cut into the part itself.

**7** Use a hobby knife to clean up any remaining roughness from the sprue attachment point. Don't try to cut too much at once—shave the material in thin slices for better control.

**8** Files large and small can also be used to clean up sprue marks and other imperfections.

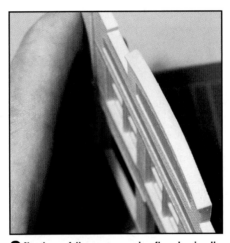

**9** No signs of the sprue remain after cleaning the area with a knife and file.

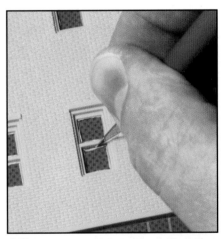

**10** Remove any mold flash with a hobby knife or files.

structure kits have a slight bevel to facilitate removal from their molds. You can use a large flat file or a sanding block, but a good tool for this task is the NorthWest Short Line True Sander (fig. 3). Figure 4 shows the sanded wall edge next to an unsanded beveled edge.

Prep all of the mating edges like this prior to beginning assembly. At the same time sand the bottom edges of the walls so they will sit flat.

Take care as you cut pieces from their molding sprues. The best way to do this is with a sprue cutter (fig. 5), but you can also chop them with a hobby knife, as fig. 6 shows. Whatever you do, don't twist or pull the parts from sprues.

Remove any leftover material from sprue cuts using a hobby knife (fig. 7) and/or files—needle files or large files,

depending on the size of the part involved (fig. 8). There shouldn't be any signs of the sprue when you're done (fig. 9).

Plastic kits sometimes have molding flash—stray plastic that creeps out of the molds—in window openings or along the sides of castings. Use a sharp hobby knife to remove flash (fig. 10).

Don't remove parts from sprues until you need them, especially on large structures with many similar-looking parts. The part identifier numbers on sprues (fig. 11) will help you quickly locate the right part and not confuse similar pieces.

## Gluing wall joints

Test-fit one of the wall joints. If there are gaps, or if the mating pieces aren't straight, sand or file the edges of the

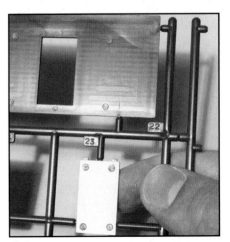

**11** Leave parts on sprues until you need them. The part numbers on the sprues make for easy identification.

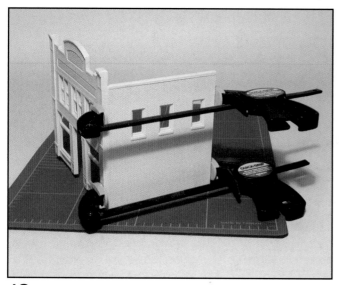

**12** Miniature bar clamps, such as these Quick-Grips, work well for holding walls in place for gluing.

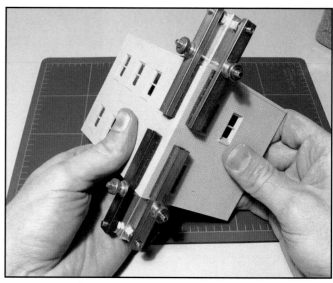

**13** These specialty clamps, called Right Clamps, are designed for holding corners together.

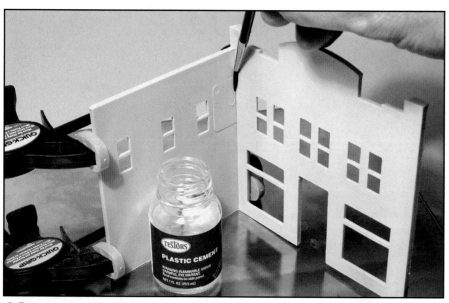

**14** Apply liquid plastic cement to the rear of the joint with a paintbrush. Capillary action will pull the glue into the joint.

**15** Apply thick plastic cement along the alignment lip inside one wall edge.

offending pieces until the joint is even and tight.

You'll need to hold the walls securely to each other to keep the joint tight until the glue sets. There are a number of ways to do this. Figure 12 shows one method, using miniature bar-type clamps such as Quick-Grip clamps. They are available in a variety of sizes and can be purchased at most hardware stores. This is the best method for heavy walls that are simply butted against each other. (You'll find these clamps handy for other modeling and layout uses as well.) They won't work well for thin or long walls.

The Right Clamp, made by Coffman Graphic Solutions Co., is another specialty clamp that is ideal for small structures (fig. 13).

Once the walls are properly aligned and securely held together, apply liquid plastic cement from behind the corner, as fig. 14 shows. Use a small paintbrush to apply the cement. Capillary action will pull the solvent into the joint. Leave the clamps in place until the joint has set securely (at least an hour; longer if possible).

Repeat the process for the other pair of walls. Once both initial joints have set, glue the remaining two joints in the

same manner, one at a time.

Many kits have alignment ridges or lips to aid in keeping the walls square, as shown on the Walthers grain elevator in fig. 15. With this kit, the wall edge is held firmly against a raised lip that runs the height of the adjoining wall. The wall with the ridge also has the corner molding, which will help hide any small imperfections in the wall joints.

To glue this type of wall, run a bead of thick liquid plastic cement on the inside of the alignment ridge (fig. 15). Don't use too much, or it will leak from the joint when the pieces are pressed together.

**16** Press the corner together, making sure the bottoms of the two walls are in alignment.

**17** Rubber bands work well to hold the walls of tall structures together.

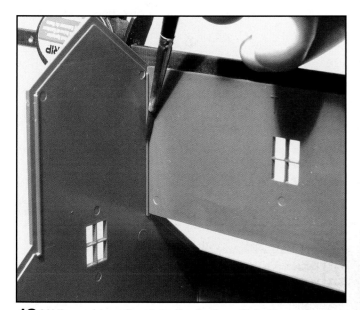

**18** Add the remaining walls and glue them in place with liquid cement.

**19** A piece of square strip styrene will help reinforce a corner joint.

When you press the pieces together, make sure the walls are in proper alignment at the bottom and top (fig. 16), and hold the joint firmly for several seconds until it begins to set. You can use clamps as well. Repeat this step with the other wall sections.

You can use rubber bands to hold the completed assembly in place until the cement dries (fig. 17). This particular kit had one side wall that was bowed slightly, but an extra rubber band in the middle was enough to pull it into alignment.

To further strengthen the joints, you can add a brushful of liquid plastic cement inside each joint after the walls have been rubber-banded together.

Once the main wall joints had set on the grain elevator, I glued the small upper walls by clamping them in place with Quick-Grip clamps and applying liquid plastic cement from behind (fig. 18).

### Reinforcing corners

If walls are thin, large, or otherwise difficult to keep aligned, the corners may need to be reinforced to keep them square.

One simple way is to glue a piece of square styrene strip into the corner, as shown in fig. 19. This works with simple butt joints, but won't work if the walls have lips or ridges along the joint. Be sure the strip won't interfere with window or door frames or with window glazing at nearby openings.

Another trick that works well, especially for larger buildings, is to use old cardboard slide mounts (fig. 20). These do a very good job of keeping joints square. You can use two or three at each corner for tall structures.

Cut off the corner to clear lips and ridges at the joint itself. Glue the mounts in place with cyanoacrylate adhesive (CA).

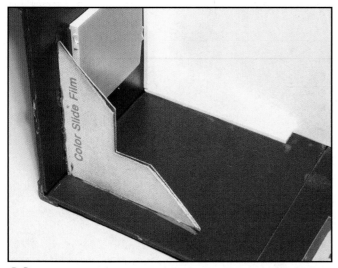

**20** Old cardboard slide mounts cut in half work well to keep corners square. Glue them in place with CA.

**21** Place drops of glue sparingly around the window opening, then carefully set the frame in place.

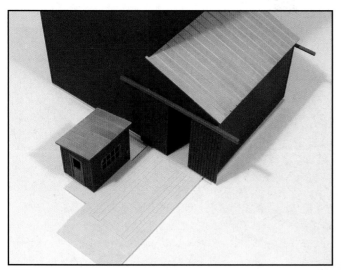

**22** The grain elevator base includes a driveway with scale detail.

**23** Ridges molded inside each wall at the top hold the nicely detailed flat roof in place.

## Window and door frames

Many plastic kits have separate window and door frames. These are designed to be glued in place in wall openings. Be careful when separating these items from their sprues, as they're often delicate because of the thin cross-sections of the frames and mullions.

Don't be too quick to install frames. Frames are often a different color from the rest of the structure. If you want to replicate that, it's easier to paint the frames separately before installing them. Chapter 5 goes into greater detail on painting.

Glue the frames in place with as little cement as possible (fig. 21). The more you use, the greater the risk that some

will ooze out the front of the opening.

Depending upon the style, frames are sometimes added from the exterior side and sometimes from the interior side. Either way I like to use just a couple of drops of thick liquid plastic cement to secure them. Add the cement to the structure, and carefully set the frame in place. Hold it for a few seconds until you're sure the cement has taken hold. Make sure the frames are properly oriented before gluing them in place!

## Structure bases

Many structures come with their own bases. I don't always use them, and when I do, I first blend the base into the scenery on the layout, then install

the structure on top of the base. Even if you don't use the kit base in your layout, it can be handy for aligning walls, especially on buildings with more than one main structure.

Figure 22 shows the base provided with the Walthers grain elevator. It has good detail, including a truck scale, so I decided to use it in my new layout. After painting the visible parts of the base, I will install it on the layout, and then add the buildings when the scenery is in place.

Some storefront-style structures use bases that include sidewalks along the front. Although at first this might seem like a good idea, the chances are slim that you'll have a neighboring structure

**24** Some roofs, such as on this DPM kit, require separate roof-support strips inside the walls to hold the sheet-styrene roof.

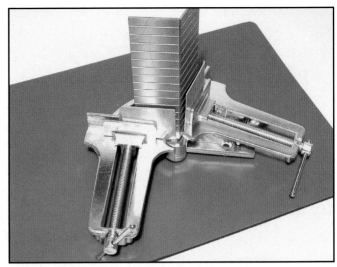

**25** An adjustable corner clamp works well for holding roof halves in place at odd angles.

**26** Pieces of cardboard protect the plastic roof from being marred by the jaws of the clamp. Apply glue to the rear of the joint.

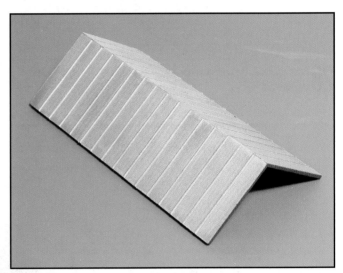

**27** The finished roof seam should have no gaps.

with the same size, style, and thickness of sidewalk. Unless you're planning to have the structure standing by itself, it's usually best to discard the base and make your own.

If you think you can easily blend the base into the scenery, then go ahead and use it; if not, do without.

## Roofs

Structure roofs come in many shapes and styles, from basic single-piece flat roofs to multi-piece peaked roofs. All must be aligned and glued with care to achieve a realistic appearance.

Flat roofs can be the simplest to install, provided you've made sure the structure is square. Some kits include

nicely detailed molded flat roofs with texture (such as stones, tar paper, metal roof seams, or other details) molded in place, as on the HO Bachmann drug store in fig. 23. Others, such as the DPM structure in fig. 24, simply give you a plain piece of styrene.

Most structures with flat roofs have ridges molded inside the tops of the walls (fig. 23). The roof piece is designed to fit atop these ridges.

If a structure kit doesn't have aligning ridges, you'll have to add your own by gluing pieces of square styrene strip in place, as fig. 24 shows. Make sure you install these at the same height on both sides of the structure. Some roofs are designed to be level, while

others slope from front to back.

The first step in installing a flat roof is to check its fit and alignment. If it doesn't fit properly, check that the structure itself is square. You may have to alter the roof slightly to get it to fit. Sand, file, or scrape away enough material from the edges of the roof so that it fits properly inside the walls.

Once you're happy with the roof's fit, you can glue it in place. If you plan to add interior detail, then set the roof aside until you're sure you don't need to get inside the structure any more.

Chapter 4 shows several methods of finishing roofs, including ways of hiding cracks or gaps around the edges of flat roofs.

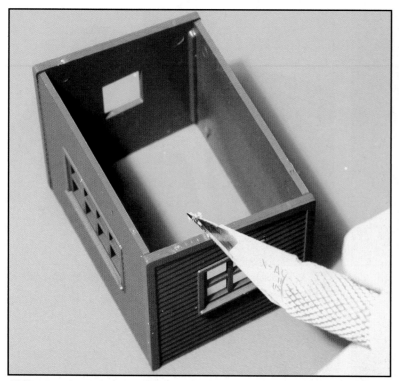

**28** Prior to gluing the roof in place, scrape any paint off of the top edges of the walls where the roof will rest.

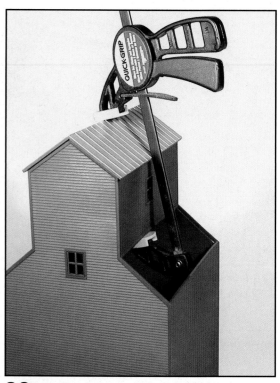

**29** If possible, clamp the roof in place on the structure before applying glue.

**30** Some kits include thick injection-molded clear styrene glazing like the piece at left. The piece at right is cut from .015" clear sheet styrene.

## Multiple-piece roofs

When working with simple (two-piece) peaked roofs, I prefer to join the two roof pieces first, then add them to the structure. I do this because the roof-peak joint is the most critical joint on the structure—any gaps appearing there will ruin the realism and appearance of the whole building. It's much easier to get a good joint at the peak when the roof sections aren't connected to anything else.

The best tool that I've found for doing this is called an adjustable corner clamp, available at hardware and home-supply stores (fig. 25). These clamps, made for holding picture frames and woodworking projects, can hold adjoining pieces at any angle and have many uses in modeling.

Place both roof halves in the clamp. Use cardboard to protect the plastic parts from the clamp's metal jaws (fig. 26). It may take some finagling to get the alignment just right, so take your time.

For small roofs, you might be able to glue the entire roof joint at once; for larger roofs it's better to glue just one end, then wait until it is completely set before clamping and gluing the other end. Use a brush to add liquid plastic cement from behind as shown in fig. 26.

When the glue is dry, check the joint for gaps. If you find any, fill them with CA. Even on tight joints, you may have to do some light sanding or scraping with a hobby knife to hide the seam line at the peak. When you're done there shouldn't be any signs of a joint (fig. 27).

Paint the roof (see Chapter 4 for techniques), but don't attach it until the structure has been painted as well. Scrape stray paint off the roof glue points on the structure before gluing the roof in place, as in fig. 28.

Test-fit the roof. If you have access to

the roof from inside, clamp or hold the roof in place (fig. 29), then add liquid cement from behind (as with wall joints). If you don't have inside access, apply thick plastic cement to one side of the mating surfaces, then carefully set the roof on the structure and place weights on top to hold everything in place.

When dealing with complicated, multi-section roofs, divide the project into subassemblies. Start with the basic roof and move on to smaller subassemblies. The key is to make sure the alignment is correct and the joints are solid at each step before proceeding.

## Window glazing

Adding clear "glass," or glazing, to your structures should be the final assembly step. Make sure the structure is fully painted and weathered to your liking before adding the glazing.

You have a couple of choices. Many kits include thick pieces of clear injection-molded plastic sized to fit the window frames of the kit (fig. 30). These pieces have the advantage of being ready to use, but their appearance is often subpar. Instead of being clear, clear injection-molded plastic is often hazy or cloudy, and its thickness is usually apparent to those looking through the window after it's been installed.

Because of this, I generally don't use injection-molded plastic unless the piece is provided in a shape unique to the building or if it is being used in an out-of-the-way area that won't be noticeable.

I recommend using clear sheet styrene instead. Clear styrene (available from Evergreen and Plastruct) is free of waviness or haziness, looks glass-like when properly installed, and comes in several thicknesses (fig. 30). I find the .010" thick material the best for general use. It's thin enough to give a realistic, glass-like appearance and it's easy to cut and handle, but it's thick enough to hold its shape without developing waves or ripples, as thinner styrene is prone to do.

The score-and-snap technique won't work on clear styrene because the plastic will craze near the break. If you need to mark clear styrene for cutting, draw a hobby knife backward across the

**31** Mark clear styrene by drawing a hobby knife backward along the surface.

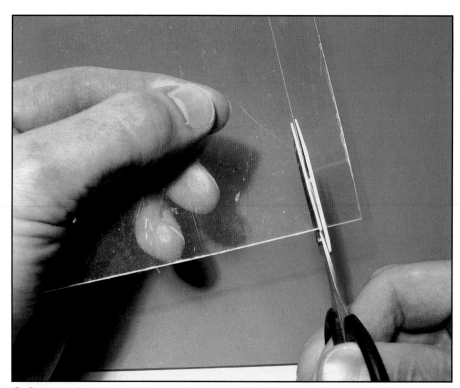

**32** Cutting clear styrene with fine, small scissors results in a clean, sharp edge.

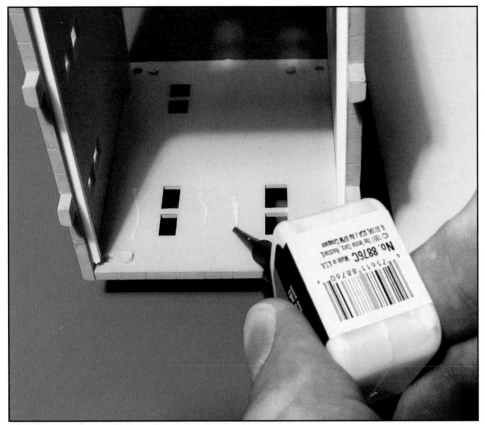

**33** Use clear parts cement to glue clear plastic window glazing in place.

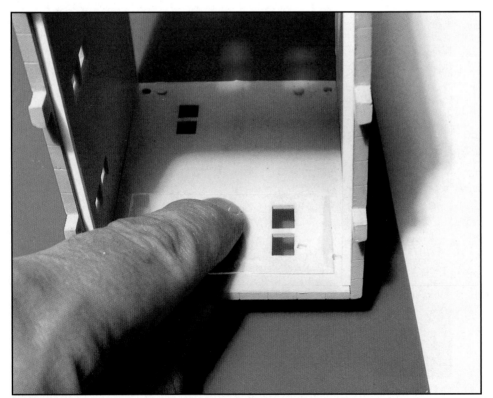

**34** Set the glazing in place carefully, making sure that the glue doesn't seep to the window face.

surface (fig. 31). Cut clear styrene with a small pair of fine, sharp scissors, as in fig. 32. The result will be a clean edge.

Clear styrene should be stored flat to keep it from warping, which makes it impossible to use as glazing. If you have plastic that doesn't lie flat, get a new piece of plastic.

The next step is gluing the clear glazing in place. Regardless of the material used, this step is critical in achieving a realistic appearance. Test-fit the glazing to make sure it fits well and is properly oriented.

As mentioned in the sidebar on adhesives (page 19), always use clear parts cement to secure glazing. This glue is cream colored when wet but dries clear and glossy, so even if a bit gets on the window surface, it will be difficult to see once it dries.

Don't use CA or plastic cement to secure clear styrene. Cyanoacrylate adhesive will fog the styrene, while any plastic cement that gets on the window surface will mark the styrene.

Apply a bit of clear parts cement to the inside of the wall or window frame (fig. 33). Make sure all four edges are secured so the glazing won't pull away and appear loose. It doesn't take much glue to achieve a secure bond.

Carefully set the glazing in place (fig. 34). Make sure it completely covers the opening. If your alignment is off and you accidentally smear glue on the window surface, cut a new piece of glazing. Press it gently until the glue takes hold. Rather than cut and place many small pieces of styrene, sometimes it's easier to cut one large piece to cover several windows (fig. 35).

Chapter 6 shows how to dress up windows with shades, view blocks, simulated interiors, and other details.

**35** Cutting the glazing into large pieces that cover several windows makes it easier to install.

# SCRAP BOX

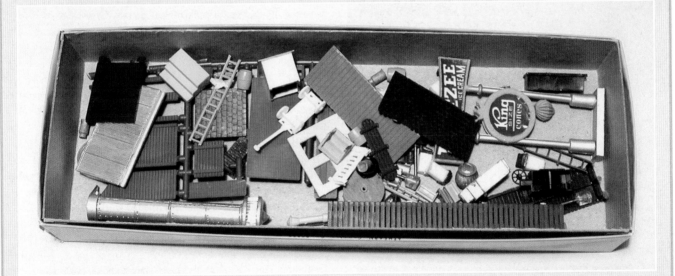

Once you start building a lot of structure kits and other models, you'll find that many completed projects result in leftover spare parts. Don't throw any of these away! Instead, start a scrap box. This is simply an accumulation of random items, including extra window and door frames, sections of walls, and miscellaneous details.

Also, if as you build new kits you "retire" older, less-realistic (or less-well-built) structures from your layout, don't just discard them. Scavenge what you can from these buildings, especially detail items such as chimneys, signs, loading docks, and roof vents (and complete roof sections if possible). You'll discover that many of them can be used later on structures or as details around the layout.

The photo above shows a number of spare parts stored in an old freight car kit box. As you build more structures and accumulate more stray items, you'll need increasingly larger boxes. You can also store parts by category, for example interior details, roof details, boxes and crates, and miscellaneous items.

# BASIC TOOLS

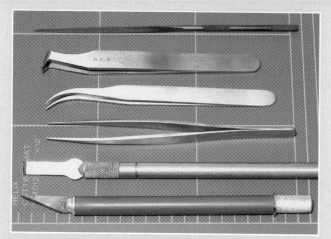

Handy tools include (top to bottom) needle files, sprue cutters, tweezers, and hobby knives with various blades.

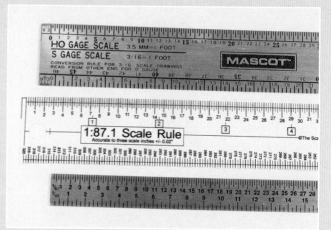

Scale rules are necessary tools for structure modeling.

Dispose of used blades in a sealed container.

Before assembling your first plastic structure kit, make sure you have the proper tools. The accompanying photos show the tools I consider to be must-haves for basic modeling.

• **Hobby knife.** First on the list is a hobby knife. I keep two knife handles handy: one with a pointed (no. 11) blade, the other with a squared-off chisel-shaped (no. 17) blade. Although you can have a single knife and swap blades back-and-forth, you'll soon find it easier to keep two separate knife handles loaded and ready to go.

Experienced modelers will tell you that hobby knives are their most-used tools. There are many types and sizes of blade handles available—find one that fits your hand comfortably. The above blades are the ones I use most often, but there are many other styles available.

Blades are relatively inexpensive (especially when bought in 100-blade bulk packs), so keep a fresh blade in your knife at all times. Dull knives will cut poorly and are much more likely than sharp blades to slip and mar models or cause injury.

Dispose of used blades properly—don't just throw them into the garbage. Buy a Sharps disposal container, or use a sealed container with a slit cut on top as the photo shows.

• **Tweezers.** Tweezers are handy for holding small parts as you attach or adjust them, or for holding two or more parts together while gluing or assembling. Tweezers should have sharp points that meet in proper alignment.

Many styles of tweezers are available. Besides standard tweezers, others you'll find useful include curved-tip tweezers (for getting into odd-shaped areas), large-tip tweezers, and reverse-pressure tweezers that will hold parts securely without requiring effort from you.

• **Files.** Large and small files are also useful. Jeweler's or needle files in various shapes, including flat, square, and round, are good for removing material from and smoothing small openings or tight areas. A large (at least 7") flat mill file will aid in cleaning long edges, such as the sides, bottoms, and tops of walls.

• **Sprue cutters.** Fine sprue nippers are a tool that I once thought of as a luxury but now consider essential. They are able to cut parts flush from their sprues with little or no cleanup needed.

You'll also find tools labeled as sprue nippers that look more like wire cutters. These are great for cutting thick sprues or chopping large pieces of plastic, but the cut edges will need to be cleaned up with a hobby knife or file when you're done.

• **Cutting mat.** The tools above are shown resting on a self-healing cutting mat, which is a great addition to your workbench. It is gentle on knife blades, and the rubber-like top surface holds work securely. Having one will save your workbench surface from a lot of cutting marks.

• **Scale rules.** Another necessary tool is a scale rule. Several types are available, including the metal 12"-long Mascot and 6"-long X-acto and 36"-long clear plastic Scale Card rules shown above. A metal rule is sturdy and serves well as a straightedge for cutting; clear rules are handy for laying across models and drawings.

# ADHESIVES

Securing plastic structure joints requires the proper adhesives. The following is a summary of cements and glues you'll find useful. The examples earlier in this chapter show how to use them properly.

### Plastic cements

The most effective glues for plastic-to-plastic (styrene or ABS) joints are solvent-based liquid plastic cements. These come either as thin liquids that must be applied with a brush, or as thicker gels that are applied with a built-in needle-point applicator.

Examples of thin liquids are Ambroid ProWeld (no. 110), Plastruct Plastic Weld (no. 2), Tenax 7-R (no. 7), and Testor's Liquid (no. 3502). Gel-type cements include Model Master Liquid (no. 8872) and Testor's Liquid (no. 3507).

Although some thin liquid cements come with built-in applicator brushes, most aren't of high quality and don't work well for precision applications. Instead, use small paint brushes (one fine, one larger), and label them for use with cement only. The brushes will make it much easier to apply cement exactly where you want it.

Use the thin liquids when you have a joint that you can hold together while the glue sets up. Add a brushful of cement behind the joint and capillary action will pull it into the joint (fig. 14).

Use gel-type cement when the surfaces to be mated are large, when you apply glue prior to clamping pieces together, or for attaching a small part to a larger one. The needle-point applicators allow precise placement (fig. 15).

Both types of cement work the same way: They melt the surface plastic on each mating piece and allowing them to fuse together. The result is a glue joint that is as strong as the plastic itself.

Here are some guidelines for using plastic cement:

• Don't use any more glue than necessary as excess glue can seep out of a joint and mar surrounding plastic surfaces.

• Use plastic cements only for plastic-to-plastic joints. They will not bond other materials.

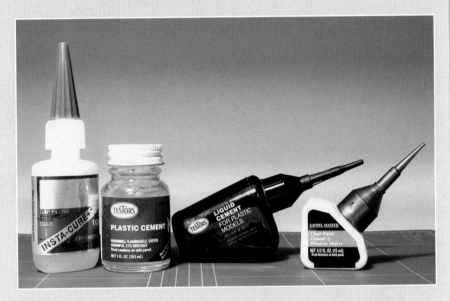

• Scrape paint away from mating surfaces prior to gluing, or the joint will not be strong.

### Cyanoacrylate adhesives

Also called super glue, cyanoacrylate adhesive (CA) is especially useful for gluing dissimilar materials such as plastic to wood or plastic to metal. Many types of CA are available, and each is handy for a different purpose.

Cyanoacrylates are rated by their viscosity, or thickness. I find medium-viscosity CA to be the best for all-around uses. It cures in 15 to 30 seconds and will fill small gaps. Examples are Insta-Cure Gap-Filling (No. 106), CGM Enterprises' Super Jet (no. 766), and Pacer Technology and Resources' Zap-A-Gap (no. 425).

Thick CA cures more slowly (30 to 45 seconds), and is handy for filling gaps. Examples are Slow Jet (no. 772) and Slo-Zap (no. 443).

Thin CA flows faster than water, cures instantly, and must be used with great care. Examples are Instant Jet (no. 761), Insta-Set Super Thin (no. 101), and Zap CA (no. 426).

For plastic kits, CA is handy for joining plastic to wood or metal or for some plastic-to-plastic joints, such as attaching small detail parts.

A toothpick is a useful tool for applying medium and thick CA. Put a small amount of CA on a scrap piece of plastic, then use the toothpick to transfer the CA to the model. It is much easier to do this than to use the applicator on the bottle.

After applying CA, you can cure it instantly using a CA accelerator such as Insta-Set (no. 151), Jet Set (no. 777), or Zip-Kicker (no. 438). These products cure CA so quickly that you don't have to clamp parts while they dry—the accelerator makes the glue set up instantly. Be aware that accelerator can remove some types of paint, so test some on an inconspicuous area before using on a finished model.

A few guidelines:

• CA has a limited shelf life, so buy the smallest bottle you need. If the CA becomes stringy or takes noticeably longer to set, buy a new bottle.

• CA will fog clear plastic. Don't use CA to glue clear plastic (or on any parts near clear plastic in enclosed areas).

• Always keep CA debonder (or acetone) within reach to free parts or fingers that become accidentally glued (especially with super thin CA).

### Clear parts cement

Clear parts adhesives, such as Testor's Clear Parts Cement (no. 3515), are the best choice for gluing clear glazing in place. Liquid plastic cement can seep quickly through a joint and mar the surface.

# KITBASHING

Kitbashing involves combining multiple kits or components into a single structure or group of structures (like a factory complex). Ed Steinberg used two

Walthers kits and a pack of DPM modular components as the basis for this small manufacturing plant. Ed Steinberg photos

You'll often hear the terms "kitbashing" and "kitmingling" used in association with building structures. The process can be as simple as rearranging the walls in a single kit, or it can involve combining parts from two, three, or more kits to

create a completely new and different building. The photos above show one example, using techniques beyond the scope of this book, but they'll give you an idea of what can be accomplished with a little creative kitbashing.

# MODULAR STRUCTURES

Modular components include various styles of wall sections, along with window and door frames, pilasters, and other details.

A steel straightedge works well for keeping wall sections aligned while gluing them together.

If you don't feel up to a full-blown kitbashing or scratchbuilding project, you can still build a custom-designed structure using modular components available from several manufacturers.

The above photo shows some of the components in Design Preservation Models' HO scale brick Modular Building System. The line (also available in N scale) includes dozens of different wall sections, with various styles of windows, doors, and blank panels. Other products available include modern prefabricated concrete wall components from Great West Models, modern corrugated-metal wall sections from Pikestuff, classic brick walls from City Classics, and industrial wall sections from Nu-Line Structures.

Before you use any of these parts it's a good idea to start by making photocopies of the components. You can then cut out, tape together, and rearrange the photocopies until you finalize the design that you're looking for.

Put the sections together like you would any other plastic kit. As you glue the sections together, be sure side-by-side wall joints are square. You can place the pieces against a steel straightedge when gluing them as the photo shows.

A finished building using DPM components is shown in fig. 17 in Chapter 6.

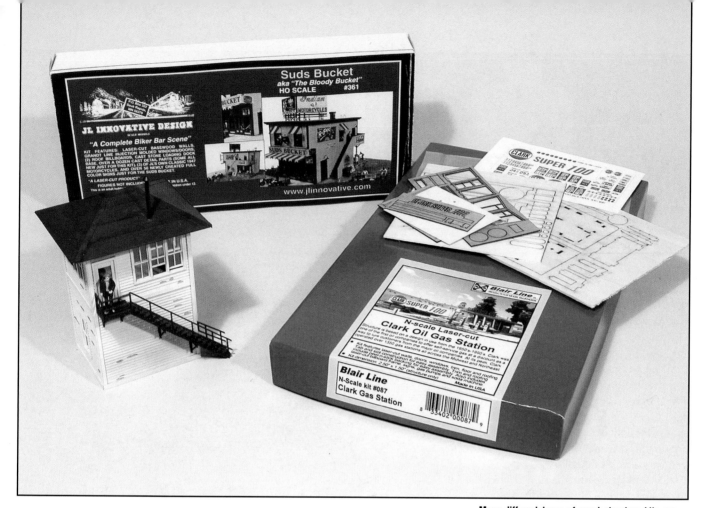

Many different types of wood structure kits are available, including (left to right) this assembled HO scale interlocking tower from American Model Builders, the HO scale Suds Bucket tavern from JL Innovative Design, and an N scale gas station from Blair Line.

# Two

# Wood kits

**W**ood structure kits have been around almost as long as the hobby itself. Over the years, wood has been used to simulate not only wood, but brick, concrete, stone, corrugated metal, and many other prototype materials. Most modern wood kits stick to representing real-life wood materials such as clapboard, board-and-batten, and tongue-and-groove siding.

Through the 1980s, the bulk of wood kits fell into what was known as the craftsman kit category. Kit walls often had to be cut to size by the modeler, and window openings would have to be cut or completed. Most detail items required fabrication by the modeler, including window frames (although many used—and still use—molded-plastic or cast-metal items for these) and other items.

Although many high-quality craftsman kits are still available, the bulk of wood kits on the market today have laser-cut components. Laser-cut parts include large items such as walls and fine details such as window frame components.

Most laser-cut components are available cut to size, with window and door openings already cut out.

Many manufacturers make wood kits in HO and N scales. Among them are American Model Builders, B.T.S., Bar Mills, Blair Line, Campbell, Durango Press, Dyna-Model Products, Evergreen Hill Designs, Fine Scale Miniatures, JL Innovative Design, Laser-Art, Northeastern Scale Models Inc., and Scale Structures Ltd.

Some of these kits feature tab-and-slot construction, which greatly aids in wall, floor, and roof alignment. Peel-and-stick wood frames and roofing materials are also common. All of these combine to make construction easier and quicker than classic craftsman kits.

**1** Glues used for wood kits include white glue, aliphatic resin (yellow carpenter's glue), and thin and thick cyanoacrylate adhesive (CA).

**2** This HO scale JL Innovative Design building (no. 361, the Suds Bucket) is typical of wood structure kits, with a mix of precut walls, stripwood, and plastic and metal window frames and details.

Wood kits lend themselves to limited-run production more than plastic kits, which need to be produced in huge quantities to cover tooling costs. Thus, many wood kits are either based on specific prototype buildings or follow a certain railroad's design.

All wood kits require painting, which takes a bit of time but isn't difficult. It can be done with a brush, airbrush, or spray can. Chapter 5 looks at methods of painting and weathering wood.

Let's look at the steps involved in assembling various types of wood kits, including gluing, cutting, and bracing.

## Basics of wood

Wood has been used for a long time for good reason: It's easy to cut, sand, and shape. It also glues readily and takes paint well. Most models use basswood, a tight-grained hardwood that is readily milled in various patterns, such as clapboard, board-and-batten, and grooved siding.

Working with wood requires different techniques from working with plastic and it takes different adhesives as well. You have a few choices with wood: White glue, carpenter's wood (aliphatic) or yellow glue, or cyanoacrylate adhesive (CA) all work well (fig. 1).

The natural grain of wood can be a benefit, especially if you're aiming for a weathered look. However, it can be a hindrance if you're trying to hide large grain patterns under a coat of paint. (More on that in Chapter 5.)

**3** The finished JL structure shows the level of detail possible with a wood kit. Seth Puffer photo

Wood requires more care in handling than plastic. Small parts—especially thin strip stock and finely cut pieces (such as windows and gables)—can break easily if mishandled. Thin walls can break if pressure is applied in the wrong place.

Unlike plastic, wood is porous. It will expand and contract with humidity, meaning test-fitting is especially important to ensure good-fitting joints. You have to take care when painting and weathering wood, as it can warp easily.

## Building a wood kit

If you've never assembled a wood kit before, start with one of the smaller laser-cut kits. Completing a project, even a small one, will give you experience in working with wood and will let you develop your wood-handling techniques.

Before beginning assembly, it's important to determine how you'll finish the structure. With wood it's often wise to paint the walls and other parts prior to assembly. If you plan to use standard paints, you can glue the structure together in subassemblies before painting, as with plastic kits.

If you're planning to stain the wood to get the look of natural, weathered wood, you'll have to stain all the parts prior to gluing anything together. You

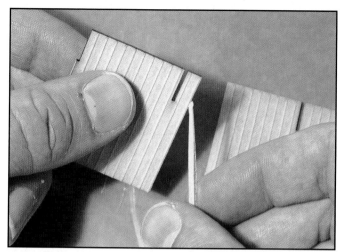

**4** If a part is broken, or if you have to join two pieces end to end, start by applying wood or white glue to one edge with a toothpick.

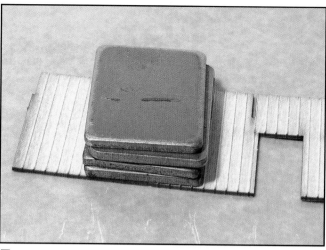

**5** Press the ends together on a flat surface covered in waxed paper, then add some weights atop the joint to keep the part flat.

**6** The repaired wall is as good as new, with no signs of breakage.

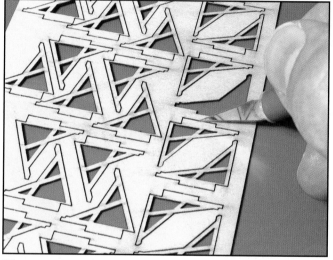

**7** Use a hobby knife to trim laser-cut parts from their wood sprues.

have to do this because stray glue on the wood surface will seal it, blocking stain from penetrating.

Figure 2 shows the parts of a typical wood kit, a small HO structure from JL Innovative Design. The kit has laser-cut walls, castings for the windows and doors, cast-metal detail parts, several sheets of color signs, and a bundle of stripwood that will require cutting for the trim and other details.

As with a plastic kit, take the time to identify all of the parts. Make sure they're all there, and that none have been broken or cracked (which happens more often with wood than plastic). Figure 3 shows what you get when the model is assembled.

If you find a broken part, don't despair. It's usually possible to repair

breaks unless the wood has splintered badly. Breaks usually happen along the grain line on thin pieces, as on the American Model Builders kit wall shown in fig. 4. To fix parts such as these, spread a very thin coat of white glue along one of the broken edges (fig. 4). Press the two pieces together firmly, then place them flat on a piece of waxed paper. To make sure the pieces stay flat, place some flat weights atop the broken pieces (fig. 5). Once the glue dries, the broken part will be as good as new (fig. 6). Use the same technique if you have a long wall and need to join wall sections end to end.

With laser kits, parts are often still attached to the large sheet from which they were cut, much like a sprue in a plastic kit. Never try to snap these parts

free—the result will usually be a broken part. Instead, use a sharp hobby knife or razor blade to separate the parts (fig. 7).

On conventional wood kits (and some laser kits) you'll have to cut wood strips to length. Many manufacturers color-code stripwood in their kits to make the pieces easy to identify (fig. 8). Be sure to cut pieces from the opposite side of the colored end.

You can trim stripwood with a hobby knife, but it can be difficult to get a square end. It's better to cut stripwood with a razor saw (made by X-acto, Atlas, Mascot, Zona, and others) and miniature miter box (from Mascot, Zona, and others), as in fig. 9.

A good tool for cutting strip material is a NorthWest Short Line Chopper (fig. 10). It will make clean, square cuts in

**8** Stripwood in kits is often color-coded to indicate size.

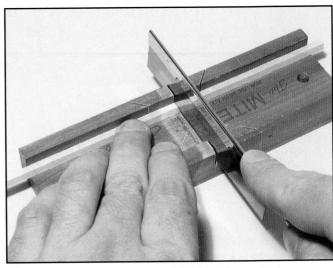

**9** A small razor saw and miter box are handy for cutting wood strips.

**10** The NorthWest Short Line Chopper works well for cutting wood and styrene.

**11** Use a knife to clean any stray material from window and door openings.

**12** After gluing, press the joint together, making sure the walls are aligned properly.

**13** This Micro-Mark gluing jig makes it easy to align walls for gluing.

wood or plastic—think of it as a miniature miter saw. If you do much model building, you'll find it to be a good investment. The razor blade in the Chopper will do a better job of cutting than a hobby knife, which has a wider blade and is more likely to mash the wood slightly at the cut.

To make sure parts are cut square, you can sand pieces using a tool such as the NorthWest Short Line True Sander (shown in fig. 3 in Chapter 1).

As with any full-sized carpentry project, a good rule of thumb is to measure twice and cut once. Although some manufacturers provide extra material in their kits, many include just enough strip material to do the job.

Making a mistake or two in cutting can mean an extra trip to the hobby shop to get more wood.

Before gluing, make sure the parts are clean and free of fuzz, fibers, and sawdust. Use a hobby knife (fig. 11) and sandpaper (220-grit and finer) to clean up rough edges. A fine jeweler's file or needle file is useful for squaring up corners of openings.

Many wood structure kits have solid floors. They help stabilize the building and keep it square—which is more of a concern with wood than plastic. They also provide a base for adding interior detailing (more about that in Chapter 6). I recommend gluing the walls together first, then adding the floor. Otherwise, if

you've glued three walls to the floor and you discover the fourth wall is too short to fit, you're stuck. If you add the floor last, you can trim it to fit without disturbing the walls.

If you've painted the walls prior to assembly, glue the window frames in place with the walls flat. If you haven't, paint them and add them after the walls have been assembled and painted.

Glue the walls together starting with one corner. If the walls have butt joints, make certain you have the right pieces overlapping, otherwise the parts you add subsequently (roof, trim, and floor) will not fit properly.

Use a toothpick to spread a thin coat of white or yellow glue along the proper edge. For small structures you can simply hold the pieces together until the glue sets, as fig. 12 shows. For taller joints, or joints where one or both walls is warped or bowed, you'll need to use a corner clamp as fig. 25 in Chapter 1 shows, or a gluing jig such as the one in fig. 13. This one, from Micro-Mark, has a metal base with right-angle edges and magnets that keep parts aligned while the glue dries.

You can also add a corner brace of square stripwood to one wall before gluing the joint (fig. 14). This gives the butt-end wall more gluing surface. If you do this, make sure the brace is glued in place flush with the end, and make sure the brace won't interfere with other interior items (such as floor, doors, windows, or roof bracing).

Some corners are designed to be exposed; others are covered with two pieces of stripwood trim forming an L at the corner (fig. 15). Yet another design has both walls butt into a square corner post—more on that in Chapter 3.

Figure 16 shows one end of a depot kit American Model Builders with the walls, floor, bracing, and some details in place. There is extra bracing in the corners as well as along the floor and walls.

## Windows and roofs

Most wood structure kits either include commercial plastic window castings or have their own wood windows that must be assembled and then installed. The plastic (or metal) castings are easy to use: Simply paint

**14** Adding a stripwood corner brace makes it easier to glue and align corner joints.

**15** The corners on some kits are covered with two pieces of stripwood forming an L, as on this American Model Builders interlocking tower.

**16** This American Model Builders depot kit shows interior bracing at the corners, along the floor, and along the inside top of each wall.

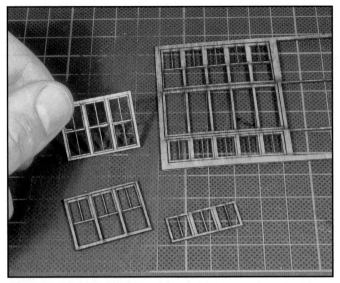

**17** Peel-and-stick laser-cut window components, such as these AMB parts, are easy and quick to assemble.

**18** The finished windows are quite realistic, as shown on this depot.

**19** Laser-cut windows can be positioned open, as on this HO scale AMB interlocking tower.

**20** Melanie Buellesbach built this HO Santa Fe depot model from an American Model Builders kit.

them and glue them in place, using small drops of medium-viscosity CA applied with a toothpick. Make sure the CA has cured before adding glazing.

The wood windows supplied in many kits are quite well detailed. The parts may look intimidating, but most have peel-and-stick adhesive backings and are fairly straightforward to put together (fig. 17). Take care that each piece is properly oriented, so that the windows will open in the proper direction.

Paint window frames before adding glazing or installing them in their openings. (See Chapter 5 for tips on painting.) Figure 18 shows a finished

window installed on the AMB depot.

Many kits have windows that can be modeled in open positions, giving buildings a lived-in appearance (fig. 19). Decide if you want to do this before assembling and painting the windows.

Roofs in wood kits are generally sheet basswood covered with various materials to represent rolled roofing, cedar shake, or shingles. The roofing materials often have a peel-and-stick backing, though some have to be glued in place. Chapter 4 offers many details on modeling realistic roofs.

Finish the structure with details and any further painting that's needed. Add window glazing, and your building is

complete. Figure 20 shows the completed HO scale AMB Santa Fe depot.

Many craftsman-level kits aren't necessarily more difficult to build than other kits, but with additional details and parts that must be cut to fit, they can be more time-consuming. Take time to make sure parts fit properly and all joints are square and solid before gluing. After you tackle a couple of simple kits, you'll be more than ready to take on a more involved project.

The next step beyond building kits is to build a structure from scratch, so let's move on and take a look at the many resources available.

Photos of the real thing were the inspiration for scratchbuilding this HO scale model of Illinois Central's Portage, Illinois, interlocking tower.

# THREE

# Scratchbuilding

Structures can be signature items on a railroad. The problem is that, unlike locomotives—where more than 100 railroads ran F7s, for example—only one of a particular prototype building may exist. If a kit manufacturer hasn't offered the building you want as a commercial model, you might consider building it yourself from scratch. Building a structure using raw materials, or from scratch, is known as scratchbuilding.

Scratchbuilding shouldn't be a scary proposition. With the wealth of raw materials available—including many styles of wall and roofing sheets, along with a tremendous variety of injection-molded plastic and cast-metal window frames, doors, and detail parts—scratchbuilding is often no more difficult than building a complex plastic kit. In fact, if you have a few plastic structure kits under your belt, you're probably ready to try a simple scratchbuilding project.

Scratchbuilding can also be a great deal of fun. I've found creating models based on real structures to be very rewarding, and scratchbuilding structures has become one of my favorite aspects of the hobby.

## Available materials

Let's start by looking at the available materials. Plastic and wood are the two dominant types, and you'll hear experienced modelers debate the merits of each. As you gain experience, you'll probably try projects using both.

Plastic is my favorite all-around model-building material. Stable and unaffected by humidity, it's easy to cut, glue, and shape, and it takes paint well. It's my choice for almost any structure that will be painted.

Wood, however, has many fine qualities, and if you're trying to capture the look of weathered or natural wood (as Chapter 5 shows), nothing does it like wood itself.

Sheets of textured building material

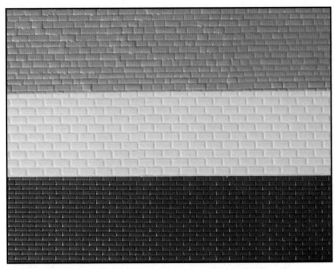

**1** Many types of textured plastic sheet are available, including (from top to bottom) Plastruct's dressed stone block (no. 91590), concrete block (no. 91620), and brick (no. 91611).

**2** Evergreen's extensive line includes many sizes of clapboard, board-and-batten, and V-groove siding.

**3** Grandt Line and others make a variety of window and door castings.

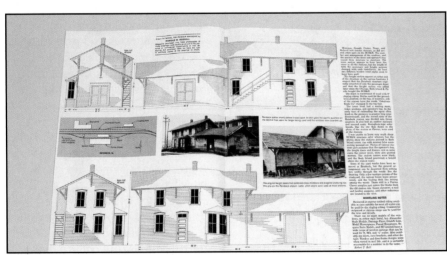

**4** Modeling magazines often publish scale drawings of structures.

are the basic building blocks for scratchbuilt structures. Plastruct, Evergreen, Holgate & Reynolds, Pikestuff, Brawa, and others make plastic sheet material for use in N through O scales. Figure 1 shows a sample of Plastruct's offerings, including brick, stone, and concrete block; fig. 2 shows Evergreen's clapboard, board-and-batten, and V-groove siding. Many sheet wood materials are also available, including clapboard, board-and-batten, and grooved siding from Midwest Products Co., Northeastern Scale Lumber, and others. These companies also make many types of sheet roofing material as well (see Chapter 4).

Windows and doors can be time-consuming to make, so if you can find a commercial part that comes close (or can be easily modified), you're wise to go that route. These are available in N through O scales from Campbell, Durango Press, Dyna-Model, Grandt Line, Micro Engineering, Pikestuff, and Scale Structures Ltd. Some are injection-molded styrene, and others are cast metal or laser-cut wood. Figure 3 shows just a few of the products available.

## Planning

You need to have a plan before you start a project. It's easiest is to start with drawings that have been published in a magazine or book. These are almost always published to scale, and the best feature of these is that all of the needed dimensions are there for you to follow. Figure 4 shows an example.

You can also design your own, either based on a real building or one from your imagination. If you're modeling a prototype building, measure it (if possible) and develop sketches showing as many dimensions as you can (height, width, and window and door sizes). Use these sketches to draw plans in the scale you're modeling. These drawings can be done by hand or on a computer.

Figure 5 shows the HO scale plans I made (on computer) for Illinois Central's Portage, Ill., tower, shown in fig. 6. When I became interested in modeling it, the building was long gone and prototype drawings couldn't be found, so all I had to go on were a few photos. This is enough to develop plans that capture the look of a building, even if some of the individual dimensions are off a bit.

To do this, estimate dimensions based on details such as door frames and siding spacing. Developing the drawings on computer allowed me to play with several dimensions and print out several versions until the proportions looked right. You don't need fancy software to do this. I simply used the basic Appleworks program that came with my Mac. Figure 7 shows the finished building in place on my layout.

Once you have plans in place, determine the materials needed, then the techniques you'll be using. How will you assemble the corners? What type of roof construction? Will you be detailing part or all of the interior? Are you using commercial windows and doors, or building your own? For the tower, I decided to use Evergreen clapboard siding and Pikestuff asphalt shingles (sheet plastic). I also decided to make my own chimney (from plastic sheet brick), doors, and windows.

Building a paper or cardboard mock-up of a building can help you verify that roof angles, wall sizes, and other dimensions are correct. In addition, it can help you judge proportions: Perhaps the roof in your design was too steep, or windows were placed too closely together. Building a mock-up will help you

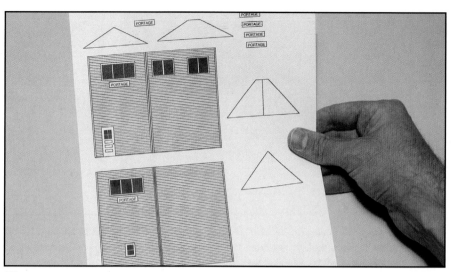

**5** These plans for an interlocking tower were developed based on prototype photos.

**6** The Illinois Central's Portage, Illinois, tower controlled the railroad's junction with the Chicago, Burlington & Quincy. Mike Nelson photo

**7** The finished model tower in the author's layout captures the look of the real thing, especially when placed in the proper scenic setting.

**8** You can draw the walls, windows, and doors directly on the sheet styrene. Use a hobby knife to score the outlines of the door and window openings.

**9** Drilling holes makes it easier to remove waste material from the openings.

**10** Bend and snap excess material from the openings.

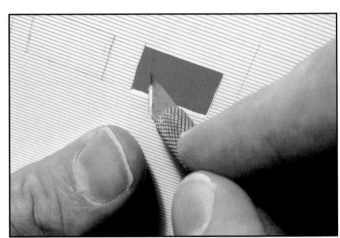

**11** Use a knife or needle files to clean up the edges around each opening.

**12** Micro-Mark's right-angle cutter (nos. 82394 and 81652) is a handy tool for cutting window openings.

**13** The easiest way to use the cutter is to mount it on a drill press (but don't turn on the drill press!) with a block of wood behind the sheet material.

**14** Using a combination square when cutting sheet material ensures a right-angle cut.

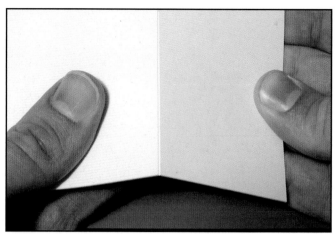

**15** Use the scribe-and-snap technique to cut plastic. After the sheet is scribed, bend it, then bend it back the other way, and it will snap in a clean line.

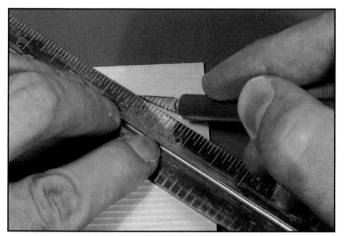

**16** When cutting sheet wood, use light cuts, making several passes until the parts are separated.

**17** Glue one wall to a square corner post. Trim the post after the glue dries.

discover any problems before you've invested time in building a complete structure.

## Putting it all together

Take the construction process step-by-step as you would in building a kit. Start by laying out the walls and window openings on the sheet material. You can draw the outlines directly on styrene with a pencil (fig. 8); it's easy to erase marks once parts have been cut out. Don't do this on wood, as the pencil marks can dent the wood, and large marks will be hard to erase.

Whenever possible, cut out the door and window openings before cutting the walls apart. This is often the most tedious part of the project. You can do

this several ways. Start by using a sharp hobby knife to outline each of the openings, as in fig. 8. You can continue making passes with the knife until the lines are cut all the way through. This is usually the best if you're working with thin material (less than .020").

You can also drill a hole or holes in the opening as fig. 9 shows. After outlining the opening with a knife, use a chisel-point blade to cut from the drilled openings to the corners, then bend and break each section of the opening away as in fig. 10. Use a knife to clean up each opening as in fig. 11.

If you do a lot of scratchbuilding, you should have a right-angle cutter, available from Micro-Mark and others (fig. 12). The best way to use this tool is

to mount it in a drill press (fig. 13). Don't turn the drill press on, but instead use it like a punch press. You can also set the tool in place on the styrene and tap it with a hammer—just make sure it's properly aligned before striking! You'll still need to clean up the opening a bit with a hobby knife.

Cut the wall sections apart as fig. 14 shows. A combination square works well for ensuring square cuts, and the heavy steel ruler provides a solid guide for the blade. The sidebar on page 34 provides some hints on working with styrene. Don't try to cut the plastic all the way through. Instead, scribe it as in fig. 14, then bend it at the scribe (fig. 15), and it will snap cleanly.

Wood can be handled in much the

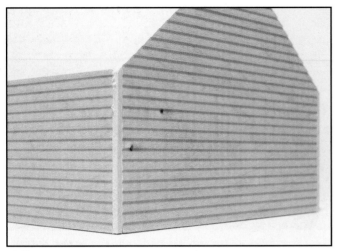

**18** When finished, the corner post looks like corner trim boards.

**19** Large structures benefit from corner bracing.

**20** Position the material on the edge of a block for stability, then use a blade to scrape material along the edge.

**21** You can also bevel an edge by drawing it along a large file or sheet of sandpaper.

**22** Taking care in beveling the edges will result in a neat, tight corner like the one shown here.

same way, but when cutting sheets, as in fig. 16, cut all the way through with the knife. Make your first couple of passes very light, then continue with moderate pressure until the cut is complete. Using excessive blade pressure, especially on the first pass, will compress the wood fibers, effectively denting the end of the sheet.

Put the walls together as with a kit, making sure that all joints are square and glued solidly together. With clapboard and other types of siding, it's easier to glue both walls to a corner post, which simulates corner trim boards.

To do this, glue one wall to a square strip (each face of the strip should be about as wide as each wall is thick). Fig. 17 shows an example with wood walls; the same technique can be used with

**23** This building has Plastruct brick exterior walls and plain sheet styrene interior walls.

**24** This panel door was made by layering two pieces of styrene after cutting the panel pattern in the top layer.

plastic. When that dries, glue the second wall in place. Chapters 1 and 2 show several ways to make sure corners are square when gluing them. The finished corner is shown in fig. 18. Large structures, such as the one in fig. 19, often benefit from additional bracing in the insides of the corners. You can also add bracing along the wall itself.

Sheets of simulated brick, block, and stone require different corner treatment. Since these materials form their own corners, they require care in getting the edges to mate cleanly. The mating edges must also be beveled.

I usually bevel with a hobby knife as shown in fig. 20. Do this by scraping—not cutting—the material. You can also use a large file or sanding block to bevel the edges (fig. 21). You don't need a perfect 45-degree angle— the bevel can be greater. The key is to make sure the outer edges of the walls meet. Check the angle frequently to make sure you don't cut too deeply. Figure 22 shows a finished joint on a structure built from Plastruct brick. Figure 23 shows the interior, which has thin sheet styrene walls and square strip styrene support braces in each corner.

## Windows and doors

Figure 3 shows just a few of the many types of commercial door and window castings available. There's a huge variety available in HO scale. N and O scale modelers also have many to choose from. If there's a commercial window or door that's close to what you're looking

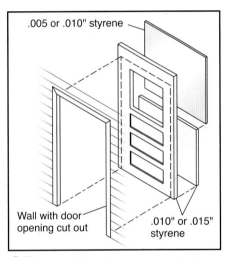

**25** Layering plain and clear styrene makes it easy to model panel doors.

for, by all means use it. You can also make your own.

Figure 24 shows an example of a door on an interlocking tower. As the drawing in fig. 25 shows, you can place two layers of styrene together to create panel doors. You can cut the panels on the top layer to make any door pattern that you need. By using thin (.010") styrene for the rear piece, the clear plastic glazing added behind it will have a realistic look (fig. 26). This technique works well for any scale.

Figure 27 shows a window and door from a brick building. The window frame is simply .010" styrene glued in place behind an opening cut into the brick material, and the door is set back from the brick wall with strip styrene. Figure 23 shows this from the inside.

**26** Here's an interior view of the door shown in fig. 24, with clear sheet styrene window glazing.

Small pins or pieces of wire work well for simulating doorknobs and door handles.

## Roofs

There's a wide variety of commercial roofing material on the market, including plastic sheets that simulate asphalt shingles, cedar shake, Spanish tile, slate tiles, and various types of metal roofing. Separate shingle pieces and strips are also available. Chapter 4 discusses these materials in depth, along with roof details.

Flat and angled roofs are fairly easy to build. Cardboard or paper mock-ups can be helpful when building hip roofs and other complex-shaped roofs. It took a few tries with mock-ups for the interlocking tower until I got the proper angles.

**27** This window frame is a single piece of styrene behind the opening in the brick layer. The door is a single piece of styrene, set back from the opening by strip styrene.

**28** The tower roof is made from four pieces of plastic roofing glued together with plastic cement and reinforced with strip styrene.

In many cases, such as the tower, making a roof is simply a matter of cutting the roofing sheet to fit (Pikestuff asphalt shingles, in this case). I beveled the mating edges with a knife and file, then glued the pieces together as in fig. 28. Small lengths of square styrene strip help reinforce the joints.

Chapter 4 goes into more detail on roof construction, and other chapters explain how to paint (Chapter 5) and detail (Chapters 6 and 7) scratchbuilt and other structures.

# WORKING WITH STYRENE

Styrene plastic is one of the most versatile modeling materials. It is inexpensive, easy to cut and handle, and impervious to humidity, and it takes paint well. Having a good working knowledge of styrene is important, whether you're scratchbuilding a structure or just making details or modifying an existing building.

Plain styrene sheets are available in thicknesses from .005" to .080", and thicker pieces are also available (although harder to find). Strip styrene is available in a variety of dimensions, as well as in rods and tubes. Structural shapes are also available, including I-beams, channels, and girders.

Styrene can be found packaged for modelers in most hobby shops, Evergreen and Plastruct being the most common brands. In addition, plastic wholesalers in mid-size to larger cities sell large (up to 4 x 8-foot) sheets of styrene—handy for large buildings or other projects. You'll find these materials used in the examples throughout this book.

The easiest way to cut sheet styrene is the scribe-and-snap method shown in figs. 14 and 15. You can also cut sheet material

Strip styrene includes channels, I-beams, tubing, plain strips, and many other shapes.

by making multiple passes with a hobby knife. Most strip material can be easily cut through with a hobby knife, but a NorthWest Short Line Chopper (shown in fig. 10 in Chapter 2) is a handy tool to have for doing this.

To glue styrene you can use any of the plastic solvents discussed in Chapter 1. These solvents melt the mating surfaces together to form a joint as strong as the plastic. Cyanoacrylate adhesive (CA) can also be used, and it's the best choice when joining styrene to other materials.

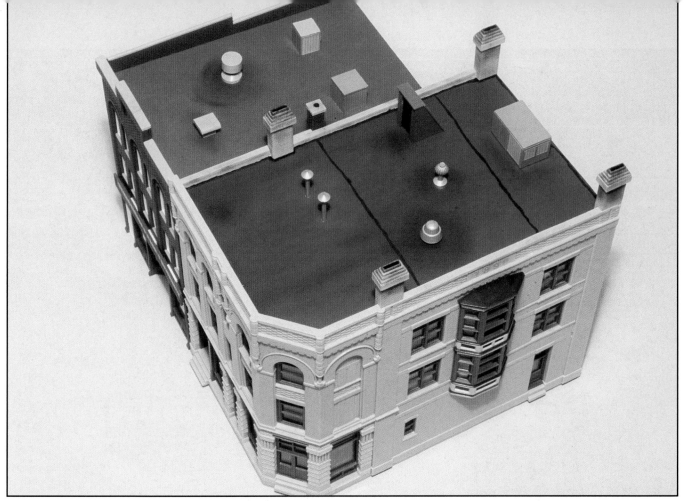

A few extra details added to the roofs improved the looks of this pair of HO scale structures from Design Preservation Models and Walthers.

# FOUR

# Structure roofs

Although most of us don't notice roofs much in real life—after all, they're generally out of our viewing range—they are quite important on model railroad structures. Why? Our perspective on all but the tallest model railroads means that we're looking down on them, which makes all of those roofs quite prominent.

Roof detail varies in quality amongst structure kits. Some kits have roofs with texture and details such as vents, chimneys, and air conditioning units; others just provide a flat piece of plastic and leave you to come up with the rest.

We'll look at the detail items that can be added to improve commercial and scratchbuilt roofs. We'll also explore some of the many roofing materials used in real life and the methods and materials that can be used to re-create them.

The roof is generally the last item to be added to a structure. Although it's possible to make some roofs removable, most are glued in place. Thus, it's important to have all windows and interior detail in place before adding the roof.

## Roofing materials and details

Many materials have been used for roofing over the years. Through the early part of the 20th century, tarpaper and other rolled roofing materials were common. Cedar shakes were often used on depots, sheds, houses, and other sloped-roof buildings. Slate shingles (often in a diamond pattern) were common for larger, fancier structures. Metal roofs of various types, including copper and galvanized steel, were also used. These could be corrugated or flat panels with raised seams. Flat roofs are often tarred, and many have crushed rock over the roof itself. Many modern flat roofs are simply smooth concrete or composite material, sloped slightly for drainage.

**1** Real buildings are loaded with details, including vents, pipes, stacks, and air conditioning units and ducts. Note the various colors of roofs on each of the buildings and the weathering effects on each roof.

Since the mid-1900s asphalt shingles have become the norm for most angled roofs. These are generally laid in a rectangular pattern and can be found in many colors, including black and various shades of gray, brown, red, and green.

Modeling these materials has become much easier in the past few years with the wide variety of injection-molded textured roofing sheets made by Evergreen, Pikestuff, Plastruct, and others. In addition, separate shingle products representing shake and other materials are made by Campbell, Evergreen Hill, and other manufacturers.

Roofs are loaded with details, as the prototype photo in fig. 1 shows. Industrial buildings have a wide variety of vents, pipes, air conditioners, blowers, and ductwork. Even small buildings have chimneys, vent pipes, television antennas, and other items.

Fortunately for modelers there's a wide variety of roof details available

**2** A wide variety of roof details is available, including sets of air conditioning units and vents from Walthers.

from many companies, including Alloy Forms, Campbell, Cibolo Crossing, Durango Press, Gold Medal Models, Great West Models, Evergreen Hill, Grandt Line, JL Innovative Design, Pikestuff, Scale Structures Ltd., Walthers,

and others. Figure 2 shows just a few of the HO detail parts available.

## Dressing up model roofs

Let's start by looking at a stock model roof and going through the steps of

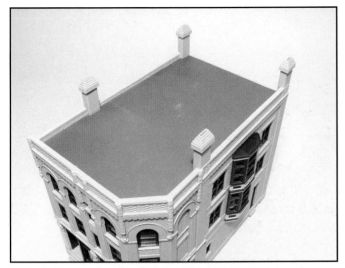

**3** This built-up structure from Walthers has nice details but a bare roof.

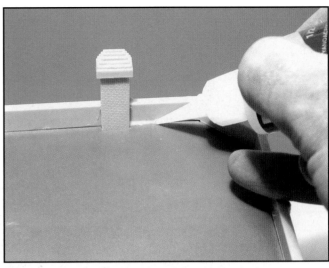

**4** Fill any gaps around the roof with a bead of thick CA.

**5** Paint the roof a dark, flat grimy black color. This is Polly Scale grimy black.

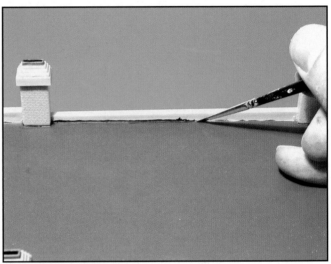

**6** Simulate a tar seam along the roof edge with black paint. As in real life, this doesn't have to be done neatly.

making it more realistic with a new finish and better details. Figure 3 shows a built-up HO scale model from Walthers, the Water Street Building (no. 933-2814). The model itself is nicely detailed, but the roof is quite barren.

Any gaps between the roof and inner walls will be quite noticeable and unrealistic. Seal them gaps by running a bead of medium CA along the joints, as fig. 4 shows. Be sure to seal the gaps around the chimneys as well.

This building has a flat roof with some texture, representing an asphalt roof. Kill the plastic shine with a coat of grimy black paint, as in fig. 5. Paint the inner walls with a color that matches the brickwork.

Use a fine-point brush and black paint to simulate the look of tar applied

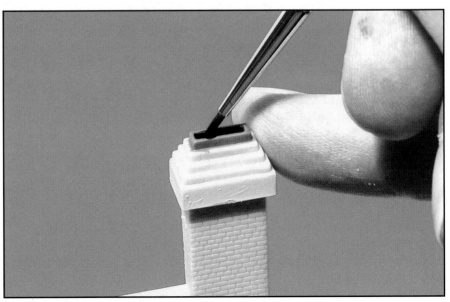

**7** Remember to paint the insides of chimneys flat black to represent soot buildup.

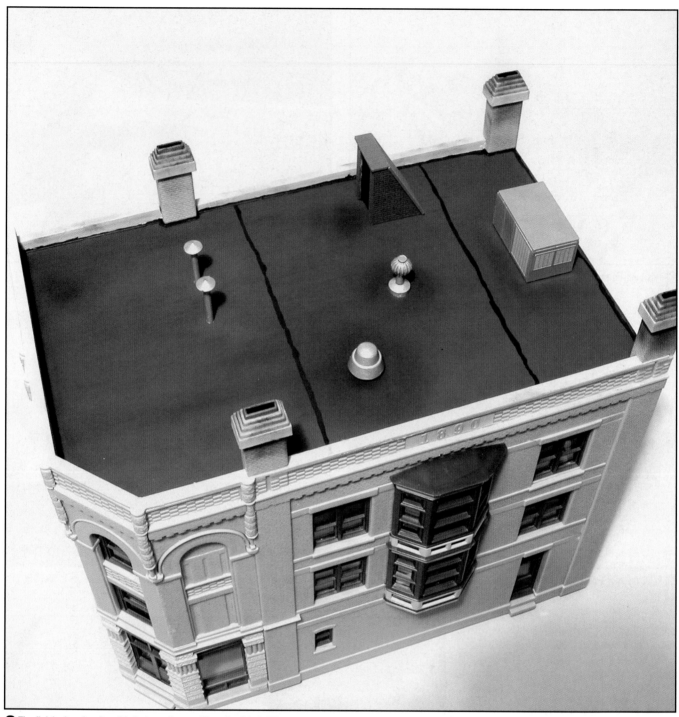

**8** The finished roof makes this look much more like a lived-in building.

to the joint between the roof and inner walls and the chimneys and roof (fig. 6). Also apply flat black paint to the insides of the chimney liners (fig. 7).

Once the roof has been painted, add other details; fig. 8 shows the finished results on the Water Street Building. The four vents (in three styles) and air conditioner unit are all from Walthers detail sets, and the stairway housing is from my spares box, a left over from an old Bachmann kit. Additional weathering includes black-paint tar seams across the roof, as well as soot around the vents and chimneys, made by brushing black powdered artist's pastel chalk in place.

Many structures have chimneys that could use some improvement. On models with solid chimneys (or when using solid cast chimney detail parts), such as the Design Preservation Models building in fig. 9, you can improve the appearance by adding a chimney tube.

Start by drilling a hole to match the diameter of the tubing you'll be using. (fig. 9). Cut a piece of brass tubing with a razor saw, test-fit it to the opening (fig. 10), paint it black or grimy black, and glue it into place (fig. 11).

Vent pipes of various sizes can be found on most prototype roofs. These are easy to make using either brass or

**9** Solid chimneys can be improved by drilling them in the center and adding piping.

**10** Test-fit the tubing in the hole before painting and gluing it in place.

**11** The finished chimneys look as if they could do their jobs much better than the solid lumps of plastic that they once were.

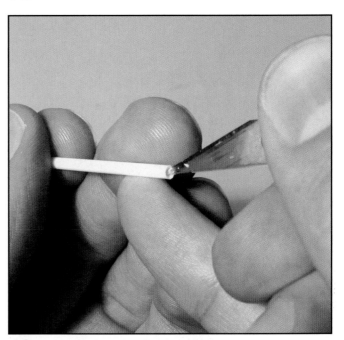

**12** Thin the walls of plastic tubing with a hobby knife.

plastic tubing. Brass tubing looks good, but plastic is easier to cut (with a Chopper or a hobby knife). The walls of plastic tubing are a bit thick in appearance, but you can easily thin them with a hobby knife (fig. 12). Carefully turn the tube while holding the knife blade steady, slowly scraping the inner wall until it has a thin profile. Paint them, then glue them in place (fig. 13).

Many industrial buildings have substantial piping on their roofs. Plastruct makes a wide assortment of pipe, fittings, and bracing. If you plan to use a lot of piping on and around structures, it's a good idea to check out the company's extensive product line. An alternative, especially if you need only a small amount of piping, is to use leftover plastic sprue (fig. 14). Sprue comes in a variety of shapes, sizes, and colors, and it serves the purpose well.

Before using sprue, scrape off any mold parting lines (fig. 15). Cut pieces of sprue to fit, paint, and install them as needed. Figure 16 shows how to drill holes where the "pipes" pass through walls and roofs. Glue the pipes from inside if possible to limit the possibility of glue showing at the joint.

Use thick CA to hide the gaps where the sprue "pipes" enter the building, then use black paint to simulate tar sealant

**13** Painted plastic tubing works well to simulate vent pipes.

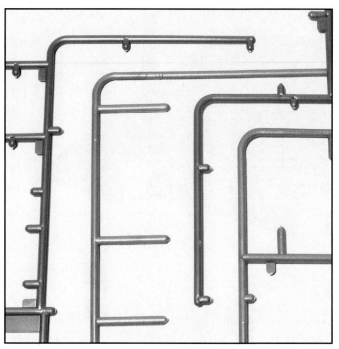

**14** Common modeling sprues often come in angles, elbows, tees, and other shapes well-suited to simulating piping.

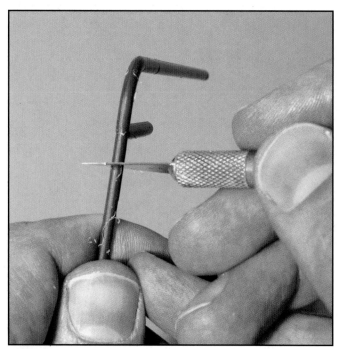

**15** Scrape off any mold parting lines from sprues before applying the paint.

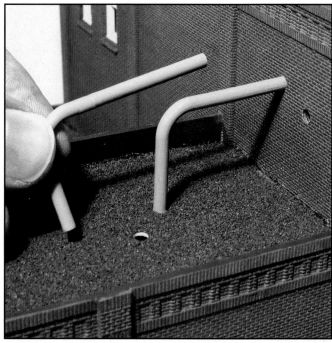

**16** Drill a mounting hole for each end of each pipe and apply glue from the inside if possible.

(fig. 17). Mars black artist's tube acrylic paint has a much thicker consistency than model paint and works well for this. Figure 18 shows the finished scene.

## Gravel roofs

Many flat roofs have crushed rock atop tar, asphalt, or other roofing material. These are fairly easy to model. Start by gluing the roof in place. Fill gaps between the roof and the sides of the building, as fig. 4 shows. Glue desired detail parts in place.

Use a wide, flat brush to paint the roof with a heavy coat of acrylic paint, such as Polly Scale or Modelflex grimy black (fig. 19). While the paint is still wet, sprinkle a generous amount of scale-sized rocks in place over the paint (fig. 20). Press the rocks down firmly

with your fingers, making sure they are firmly pushed into the paint (fig. 21). The dark paint will look like tar if any of it shows through the layer of crushed rock.

When the paint dries it will act like glue, holding the crushed rocks firmly in place (fig. 22). Once the paint is dry, turn the structure over and pour off the excess ballast, saving it for future use. For large

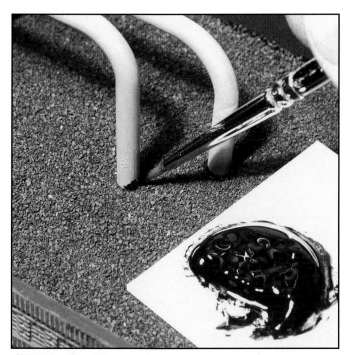

**17** Thick black artist's acrylic paint works well for simulating tar sealant around the spots where pipes enter a structure.

**18** The finished sprue pipes lend an extra touch of realism to the building's roof.

**19** Give the roof a heavy coat of gray acrylic paint such as Polly Scale grimy black.

**20** Give the roof a heavy coat of grimy black paint, then sprinkle ballast in place over the wet paint.

**21** Press the ballast firmly into the paint before the paint dries.

**22** The wet paint acts like glue, neatly holding a layer of rocks in place.

roofs, work in sections so you can lay down the ballast before the paint dries.

Ballast works well for roofing material. You can use any number of colors, from gray and black to browns and tans. Use extra fine or fine ballast for N scale; fine or medium for HO; and medium or coarse for O and larger scales.

## Rolled roofing

Tar paper and other rolled-material roofs are among the easiest to model—all you need is a smooth surface as a base. For the roofing to appear realistic, it must be made from something thin. I've found tissue paper or single-ply paper towels to be the best. These

materials can vary among brands, so test them for appearance before using them on a model.

For my example, I used facial tissue (don't use the types that have lotion added). Most facial tissue is two-ply, so separate the layers before using. You can do the same with paper towels, either separating the layers or using single-ply. Be sure you use non-embossed material.

Cut the tissue into strips a scale 36″ or 48″ wide (fig. 23). Don't worry if the width varies slightly; real tar paper often varies the same way. The material can be hard to handle, so use a fresh hobby knife, and use a straightedge to press down firmly on the tissue as you cut it. Cut the strips so they are an inch or two longer than the roof they are going on.

Brush the lower part of the roof (an area about two strips wide) with a thin coat of grimy black acrylic paint. While the paint is still wet, lay a strip of tissue paper at the bottom of the roof, as in fig. 24. Pull the strip tightly lengthwise as you lay it in place. This will keep it straight and make it easy to align. Press it lightly into place (fig. 25).

Continue the process, adding succeeding strips of paper while slightly overlapping the previous ones below it, until the roof is covered.

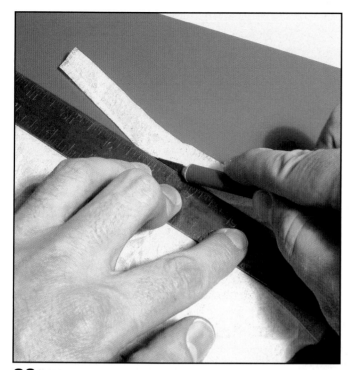

**23** Hold tissue firmly with a heavy steel rule and cut it with a hobby knife, with the blade held at a low angle to the tissue.

**24** Pull the tissue strip tightly to straighten it, then lay it atop the wet paint.

**25** Press each strip lightly with your fingers to secure it in place

**26** Once the layers are all in place, give the whole roof a coat of paint.

Once the strips are all in place, let the paint dry. Brush the roof with another light coat of grimy black paint (fig. 26). The finished roof is shown in fig. 27. An easier variation of this technique is to simply use large pieces of tissue instead of strips. You'll lose the seam effect of the strips, but the texture will still be effective.

### Shake shingles

Cedar shake shingles on roofs were common through the mid-1900s and can still be found on many new structures where the owner wants a retro look. Shake shingles are found in different sizes, and since they're a natural material each has a different look.

Sheet material is available from Dyna-Model, Plastruct, and others (fig. 28), and is included in most plastic kits that have simulated shake roofs. However, I think individual shingles, like those made by Evergreen Hill Designs (fig. 29), are the most realistic. These are laser-cut from real cedar and have a peel-and-stick backing for easy mounting.

Start by weathering the shingles

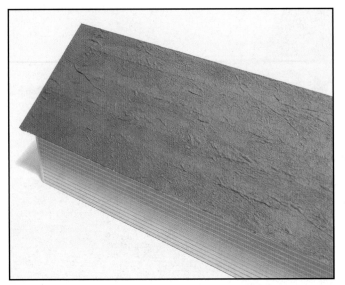

**27** The completed roof has the texture and look of rolled tarpaper.

**28** Plastic sheets of simulated shake roofing are available from Dyna-Model (shown) and others.

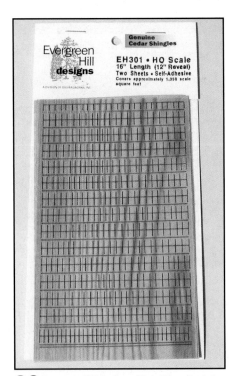

**29** Evergreen Hill Designs offers HO scale shakes made from real cedar.

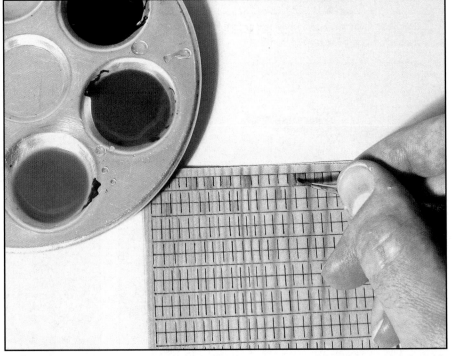

**30** Weather the shakes them before installation. Here, the author applies a light wash of artist's acrylic paints. Different colors will be applied to different shingles to vary the overall appearance of the roof.

(fig. 30). I did this, as Chapter 5 explains, by mixing washes of artist's acrylic paint (black, burnt sienna, and raw umber) and applying them to the shingles. Give some areas of the sheet an overall wash, then highlight individual shingles with various colors. You can vary the effects, from light for a new roof to heavy and dark for an old, weathered roof. Let the paint dry before proceeding.

After cutting the strips from the sheet, trim the bottom of some of the shake

shingles at different angles (fig. 31). You can take this to any extent, cracking and removing a large percentage of shingles to simulate an old roof.

Apply the strips starting at the bottom, making sure to vary the location of the joints between strips. Peel off the backing paper to expose the adhesive (fig. 32) and press the shingles in place (fig. 33). You can do additional weathering once the shingles are in place. Figure 34 shows the finished roof.

If you're working with sheet material, as in fig. 28, you can approach weathering the same way, but with paint instead of washes. Start with a brown, tan, or grimy black base coat, then paint individual shakes with various colors.

## Asphalt shingles

Asphalt shingles have become the most common roof covering on angled roofs. Unlike shakes, asphalt shingles have a consistent pattern that doesn't

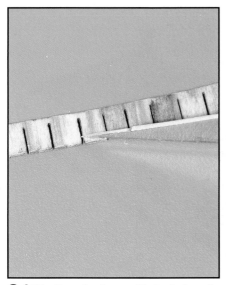

**31** Trim the ends of some shingles to keep the rows from looking too uniform.

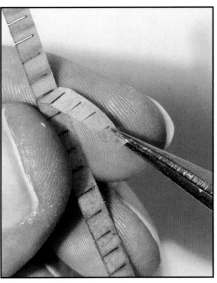

**32** Use tweezers to carefully peel the backing paper off the shingle strip.

**33** Place the strips, varying the positions of the joints between shingles. Press them down firmly when they're in place.

**34** The finished shake roof has a realistic varied appearance. This example has been lightly weathered to represent a fairly new roof.

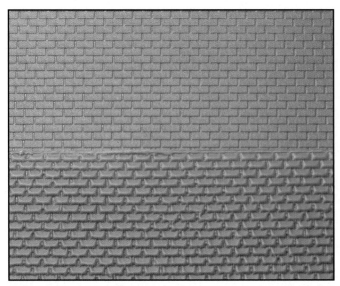

**35** Both Pikestuff (top) and Plastruct make plastic sheets of simulated asphalt shingles in HO scale.

**36** This HO house from Atlas has a shiny, plastic-looking roof with molded-in shingle texture.

**37** Give the entire roof a coat of a flat color, such as grimy black, to kill the shine of the plastic.

**38** Once the roof is painted, highlight individual shingles with slight variations of the base color.

vary much. Many plastic models have roofs with shingle texture molded in place; sheet material is also available from Plastruct, Pikestuff, and other companies (fig. 35).

Real shingles can be found in almost any color, including black, dark and light gray, and various reds, browns, and greens. Figure 36 shows an assembled HO house from Atlas with a simulated shingle roof. The first step in making a realistic shingle roof is to kill the plastic shine with a coat of flat paint—Polly Scale Grimy Black in this case (fig. 37).

Many real shingles have slight variations in color. Capture this look by using a brush to highlight individual shingles with different colors (fig. 38). To do this, start with a few drops of the base color, then add just a bit of white or black paint to vary the shade. Figure 39 shows the finished roof.

## Metal roofing

Several types of metal roofing can be found on structures. Most are either flat panels joined with raised seams, or sheets of corrugated galvanized steel. Most models with simulated metal roofing have roofs of injection-molded styrene, molded in silver. Plastic sheets of textured roofing are available from

Brawa, Evergreen, Plastruct, and others.

Some kits include pressed-metal corrugated material (generally aluminum), which is also sold separately by Campbell Scale Models (fig. 40).

These materials can all be treated much the same way. Regardless of their initial color, painting will give the roofs a more realistic appearance. Start with a base coat of a color like Polly Scale flat aluminum. This can be airbrushed or brushed—if you use a brush, keep your strokes in the direction of the ridges or grooves. Any brush marks will simply look like weathering (fig. 41).

The roof from the HO scale Walthers

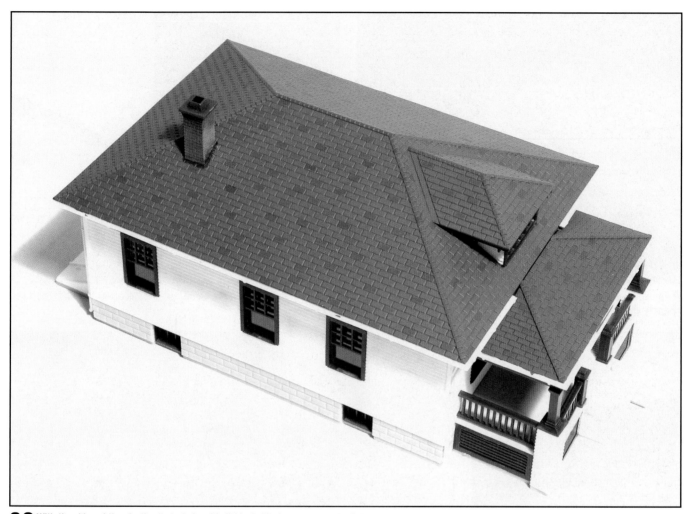

**39** With the shine of the plastic eliminated and individual shingles accented, the finished roof has a much more realistic appearance.

**40** Campbell Scale Models makes corrugated metal sheeting in various widths.

**41** Polly Scale flat aluminum is a good base color for simulating galvanized metal. Brush it on parallel to the groove or ridges of the roof surface.

elevator kit in fig. 42 consisted of thick pieces of silver plastic with raised-seam texture. After painting the roof surface silver, I painted the edges boxcar red to match the structure. This was to make the edges look like trim boards, which is a handy technique to use if the roof itself is fairly thick. Scraping the corners with a knife as shown in the photo cleans the paint line, giving the appearance from a distance that the roofing material is a separate layer.

Galvanized metal has a metallic, dull gray look. You can tone down the bright silver color by brushing powdered chalk pastels over the surface (fig. 43). Browns (simulating rust), grays, and black work well. The finished roof is shown in fig. 44.

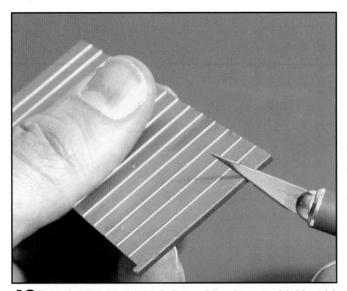

**42** The roof surface is painted dull silver, and the edges are painted to match the structure color.

**43** Powdered chalk in black, brown, and gray works well for weathering metal roofs.

**44** The finished roof appears to be in good shape, but with enough weathering to make it look as if it's been there for a few years.

**45** Campbell's corrugated metal appears realistic both on a roof and as building sheathing.

Figure 45 shows a corrugated metal roof on a scratchbuilt structure. The roofing is Campbell's corrugated metal, cut into sheets. The thin profile gives it a realistic look. I airbrushed the panels flat silver before attaching them to the roof, then gave the whole roof a wash of thinned grimy black paint (about one part Polly Scale grimy black and 10 parts Polly S airbrush thinner). The result is a dull metallic color close to galvanized metal.

The rust patches are streaked on with various rust-colored paints (such as Polly Scale Rust or Roof Brown, and artist's acrylics such as burnt sienna),

along with powdered pastels. You can paint small patches as the photo shows, or entire roof panels (or entire roofs) to simulate well-worn roofs. Chapter 5 covers painting and weathering in more detail.

## Realism is the key

Study structures in real life, along with photos and photos in books. Take note of the types of roofing used and the features used. Don't treat all of your model structures with the same roofing techniques: Vary the colors and styles of roofing, and use different types of details on each building.

Use the many available detail parts to dress up your model roofs. Also, keep in mind that an easy way to radically change the appearance of a commercial structure (kit or assembled) is to change the roofing material. For example, applying a corrugated metal roof over the shingles on a grain elevator kit can effectively backdate it; likewise, applying shingles over a shake roof can modernize an older building.

We've now looked at some painting and weathering techniques for roofs. The next chapter will explain ways of painting and weathering the structures themselves.

There are many techniques to painting realistic structures, such as the brickwork on this HO scale drugstore from Bachmann.

# FIVE

# Painting

Nothing will improve a structure's appearance more than a good paint job. Even the most beautifully crafted, highly detailed building will not look good if it has a poor paint job, or—in the case of plastic buildings—no paint at all. We'll look at various methods of painting to re-create different surfaces, including brick, wood, tin and corrugated metal, and various types of siding.

Many plastic structure kits (and assembled structures as well) tout that they're molded in realistic colors, or that no painting is needed. Don't believe a word of it. Plastic is a fantastic modeling material that will hold extremely realistic textures, but regardless of color, bare plastic looks like one thing: plastic.

When you're building a kit, first determine the colors you would like it to be. This includes the main walls, window and door frames, roof, and any other items such as cornices and iron structure fronts. Look at buildings in real life to get ideas for painting and weathering. Books with color photos are also helpful guides if you're looking for realistic colors for structures and details.

The best way to approach painting, as mentioned in Chapters 1 and 2, is to paint structures in subassemblies whenever possible. Let's start with a look at painting brick.

## Painting brick

From lineside industries to downtown storefront buildings, many structures are made of brick. Therefore, it's important to be able to simulate realistic brick finishes.

Although we often think of brick as simply being red, it comes in many colors, including shades of brown, red, cream, and tan, to name a few. Many buildings have bricks that are the same basic color, while others have bricks that vary widely in shade (fig. 1).

**1** Brick and mortar come in many colors and shades.

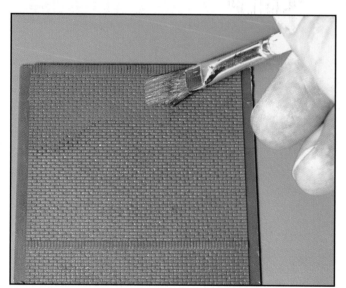

**2** You can paint brick buildings with a brush, airbrush, or spray can.

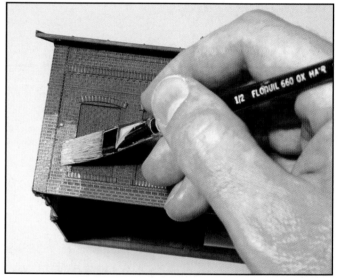

**3** Apply the mortar wash with a wide, flat brush.

Brick can be a challenge to paint because we also have to consider the mortar color. Study prototype buildings for examples. Mortar is generally not bright white, but a shade of gray or off-white that often ranges toward the color of the bricks themselves. Another twist is that brick walls are sometimes painted, making the whole wall a uniform color.

Most models that simulate brick are injection-molded styrene (sometimes resin or plaster in craftsman kits). Injection-molding capture the texture

and style of bricks well, but it doesn't matter what color they're molded in—plastic has to be painted.

Several techniques can be used to paint realistic brick finishes. I've had success with each; I suggest giving them all a try to see which one works best for you. Each will provide a slightly different appearance, which can be used to add variety to your structures.

Let's start with the color. There are so many shades of brick that it's hard to go wrong. If you're not sure, start with a

shade of boxcar red or dark red. Stick with flat paints.

I use acrylic paints almost exclusively. Today's acrylics, such as Badger Modelflex and Polly Scale, are easy to use and adhere well to plastic and other modeling materials. Acrylic paints are easy to clean up with water, leaving no worries about paint fumes as with solvent-based paints. Don't worry about brand—base your choice on the color you're looking for.

Good brick colors include Polly Scale

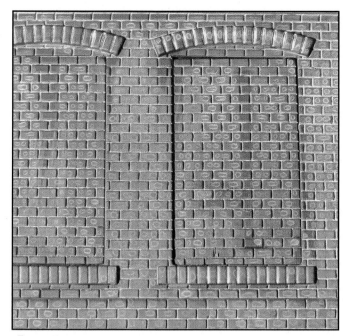

**4** With the wash technique, some of the mortar color will creep onto the brick surface.

**5** A pencil eraser will remove most of the mortar color from the brick face.

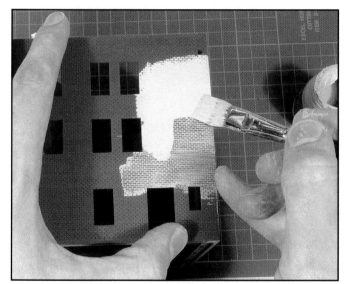

**6** Working in small sections, paint the mortar color over the brick. The section below shows the results after wiping off excess paint.

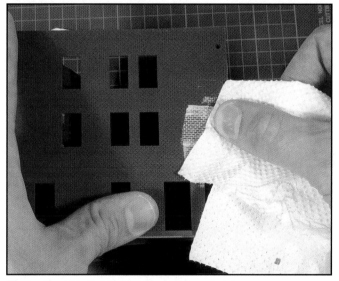

**7** Wipe the paint off of the brick faces using a soft cloth.

railroad tie brown (no. 414329), roof brown (no. 414275), boxcar red (no. 414281), oxide red (no. 404079), and special oxide red (no. 414354). Modelflex dark Tuscan oxide red (no. 1613), light Tuscan oxide red (no. 1614), and maroon Tuscan oxide red (no. 1615) also work well.

Painting walls after assembly makes it easier to hide joints, but depending on how the kit is laid out, it may be easier to paint before assembly and touch up the joints later.

## Brick with mortar wash

Begin by painting the entire building with the base brick color, then add the mortar color using a thinned wash of mortar-colored paint.

You can use a brush or airbrush for the base coat. I prefer an airbrush because it is faster and gives a smooth, even coat of paint, but a brush will also work just fine, as fig. 2 shows. Use a wide, flat brush, and be sure to work the paint into all of the cracks, crevices, and mortar lines. Because of the brick texture, you don't

need an ultra-smooth coat of paint. Let the paint dry thoroughly and add a second coat if needed.

The next step is to add the mortar color. If in doubt about what color to choose, start with medium gray. You can also mix in some of the base brick color that you used. Thin this paint with Polly S Airbrush thinner (about 10 percent to 20 percent paint and 80 to 90 percent thinner). Water will also work, but it will tend to bead up on the model's surface. The alcohol-based airbrush thinner has a

**8** Work powdered chalk into the mortar lines with a large, soft brush.

**9** The finished wall has the mortar lines accented and a weathered, dusty appearance.

**10** Use the flat area of a wide brush to pat the brick color on the brick faces only.

**11** Giving the building an overspray of the thinned brick color tones down the starkness of the mortar color.

lower surface tension and will flow more readily into the mortar lines.

Apply the wash with a wide, flat brush (fig. 3). Make sure the structure side is flat as you do this, or the paint will not cover evenly. Don't forget to cover all the mortar lines, and be sure to let each side dry thoroughly before moving to the next wall.

When the mortar paint dries you'll sometimes find that some of the mortar color has dried on the brick surface (fig. 4). Normally, this isn't objectionable, as

it can give the bricks a nice weathered look. However, if you think too much of the color has crawled on top of the bricks, you can remove some of it using a pencil eraser, as in fig. 5. Just rub lightly until the mortar color goes away (since it's a wash it won't stick as well as undiluted paint). Don't rub too hard, or you may remove the brick color as well.

### Mortar paint-and-wipe

A variation of the above method is the paint-and-wipe technique. To do this,

start by painting the structure a brick color as above.

Choose or mix a mortar color, but don't thin the paint. Working in small areas, paint the mortar color on the brick wall (fig. 6), then use a cloth to wipe the paint off of the brick faces (fig. 7). Keep working in small areas until the wall is finished.

This technique works best on walls with deep mortar lines, and for structures where you're looking for a more heavily weathered appearance.

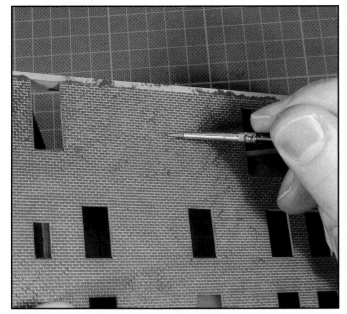

**12** Highlight individual bricks with various shades of red.

**13** Mask the gluing areas of window frames before painting them.

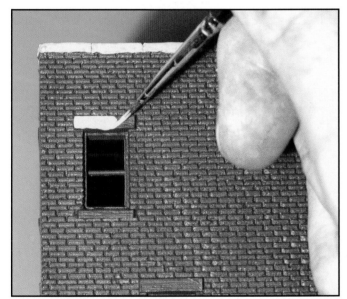

**14** Paint molded-on details using a fine-point brush.

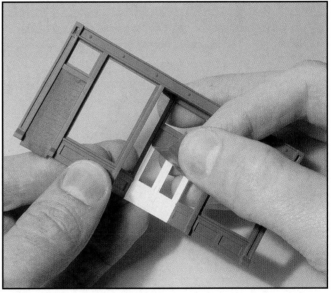

**15** You can paint doors and window framing first, then mask them and paint the surrounding color.

## Pastel chalk powder mortar

You can also use powdered chalk to simulate mortar. Use powder scraped from artist's pastel chalks, combining several shades of gray mixed with black and white (and sometimes red or brown) until you have the shade of gray you're looking for.

Apply the powder to the surface with a wide, soft brush (fig. 8). Work it into all of the mortar lines across the entire surface, then brush the surface lightly on a diagonal pattern to rid the brick

surface of most of the powder. The finished wall is shown in fig. 9.

Add a light coat of clear flat finish to seal the pastels. I prefer Polly Scale flat finish sprayed from an airbrush. If you use a spray can, try Model Master clear flat. (Some modelers prefer Testor's Dullcote from a spray can, but I find that consistent results can be hard to achieve with it.)

The key to this technique is that the wall must be painted with a flat paint. If the surface is satin or gloss paint (or

worse, raw plastic), the chalk won't stick—especially after spraying it with clear flat.

## Mortar color first

A third technique—and one I've had a great deal of success with—is to start with the mortar color first, followed by brush-painting the brick color. Start by airbrushing or brush-painting the entire building with your choice of mortar color. Let the paint dry thoroughly.

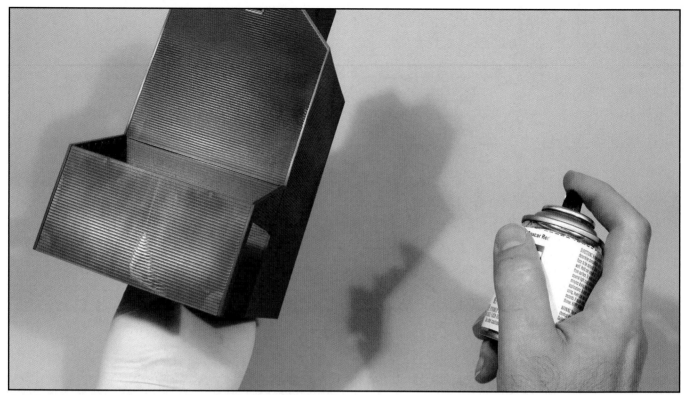

**16** Spray cans work well, especially for large structures. The paint comes out quickly, so keep the can moving. Wearing latex rubber gloves will help keep the paint off your hands.

**17** A smooth, even finish can be achieved with a spray can.

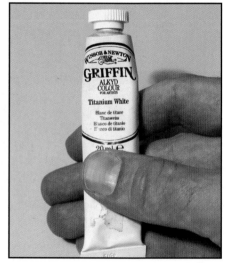

**18** Artist's alkyd color (white) works well for adding stucco texture to walls.

Next, use a wide, flat brush to dab the brick-colored paint on the walls (fig. 10). The key is to use the flat area of the brush to pat the brick faces. Don't use ordinary brush strokes, or the brick paint will go into the mortar lines.

An optional step that can also be used with the other techniques is to airbrush the entire structure with a light coat of thinned brick color (about 20 percent paint and 80 percent thinner). This will give the structure an even appearance, and effectively tone down the mortar color if it is too stark (fig. 11). You can also accomplish this with a wash, but it's more difficult to control the results.

## Individual bricks

You can stop at this point and have a realistically painted brick building, but with a few minutes of extra work you can give your structure a superdetailed appearance.

As noted above, many buildings use bricks of varying shades. To give a model this appearance, use a fine-point brush to highlight individual bricks with two or three additional colors (fig. 12).

At first glance it might seem as if this would take a great deal of time, but the

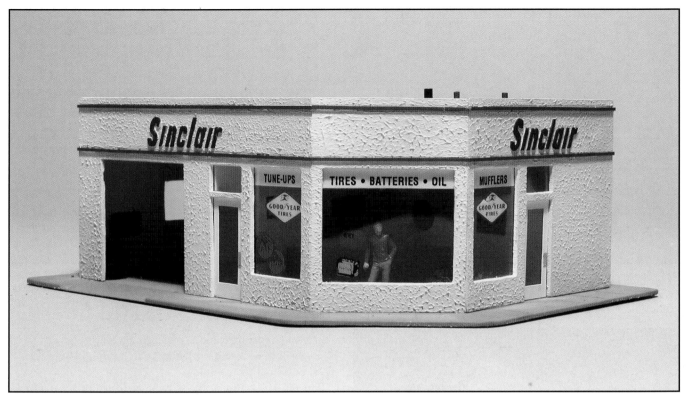

**19** Artist's alkyd color stippled on the walls gives this scratchbuilt HO gas station a stucco appearance.

**20** To create a stippled finish, dab the brush vertically into the paint and pull straight up.

**21** Common household acrylic primer also works for priming wood models.

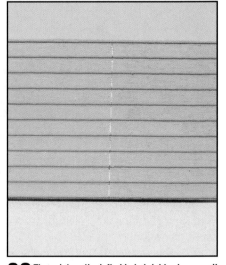

**22** The paint on the left side is brighter because it was applied over a coat of primer. The wood grain is more prominent on the right, where Primer was not used.

process actually goes quickly. And the results can be striking, as the photo on page 49 shows.

## Windows, doors, and trim

If the kit you're building has separate pieces for the windows, doors, cornices, and other trim items, paint them before attaching them. Add strips of masking tape over the rear tabs that will be glued

(fig. 13) before painting. An airbrush (or spray can) is by far the fastest way to paint window frames and other intricate items. As fig. 13 shows, keeping the parts on their sprues (if possible) speeds the process.

Often these items are molded in place on the walls. Paint the walls first, then paint the details using a small brush as fig. 14 shows. Window frames

are often white but can be found in a variety of other colors, as can cornices and trim. Window opening headers and footers are usually concrete or stone; they can be painted light gray, tan, or a concrete color.

A quicker way to paint molded-in-place window frames, doors, and mullions is to airbrush or spray paint

**23** Primer goes on well with a brush. Make sure all areas of the structure are covered.

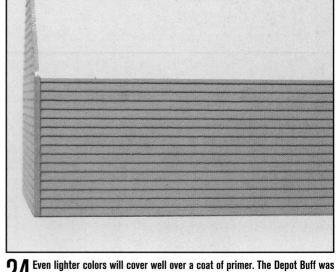

**24** Even lighter colors will cover well over a coat of primer. The Depot Buff was brush-painted.

**25** Painting wood on both sides limits warping and and future changes due to humidity.

them before painting the walls or surrounding areas. Cut squares of masking tape, place them over the frames, and paint the walls.

Once the walls are done, peel the tape away (fig. 15). The result is neatly painted windows and doors with a lot less hassle than painting them individually with a brush.

## Clapboard and other wood siding

Clapboard and board-and-batten are among the most common wall surfaces. Painting is a straightforward task using an airbrush, spray can, or brush.

When brush-painting, use as wide a brush as practical and brush in the direction of the siding using as few strokes as possible. Once the paint is on, leave it alone. Apply another brushful of paint to a nearby unpainted area, and brush the new paint back to the wet area. Try to keep the edges wet to avoid overlap marks.

When brush-painting, it often takes multiple coats to

achieve a good appearance. If your final color is light (such as white, yellow, or bright red), it helps to apply a light gray or silver base coat first.

You can also paint siding with an airbrush or spray can (fig. 16). I used Floquil boxcar red spray paint on this Walthers grain elevator. Don't apply a heavy first coat—keep the spray can moving. Spray in a back-and-forth pattern, slightly overlapping each pass. Let each coat dry thoroughly before adding the next one. These methods result in very smooth, even finishes (fig. 17).

## Stucco

Some structures have a stucco or stippled finish. You can re-create this effect on models using tube paints. I've had good luck simulating stucco with titanium white alkyd color (fig. 18). Used mostly by artists, alkyd paint has a quicker drying time (about a day) than oil colors, and it sticks well to most materials, including plastic.

The scratchbuilt Sinclair gas station in fig. 19 shows the results of this technique. Roughing up the plastic a bit with fine sandpaper (220-grit) will help give the paint some "tooth" to hold onto. It's also important to make sure the surface is very clean. Wash the plastic, scrubbing it with a toothbrush and some liquid dish detergent. Rinse it thoroughly and let it dry.

Brush the alkyd paint onto the surface. A thin coat is all that's needed, but make sure the entire surface is covered. Use a stiff brush (a round hog bristle brush is ideal) to stipple the surface (fig. 20). Press the brush vertically into the paint, then pull straight up. Repeat until the entire surface is textured.

You have about 24 hours before the paint dries, so you have quite a bit of time to get the right effect. Let the paint dry completely, then repeat the process for the other sides of the structure. Once the alkyd color is dry, you can paint it to tone down the bright white of the tube paint.

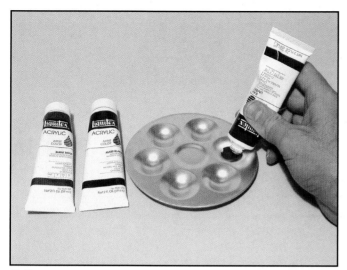

**26** Squeeze a bit of each color of acrylic paint onto a small palette.

**27** Add water and stir each color using a small stick.

**28** Use a brush to apply the thinned colors.

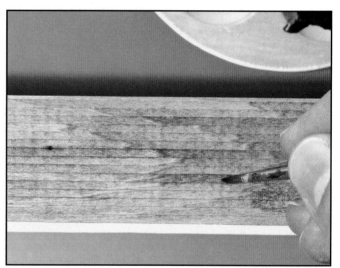

**29** A small brush works well for highlighting individual boards.

## Painting wood

Many of the techniques are the same for wood as for plastic. The biggest difference is that wood is a porous, grained material that will soak up the paint, which makes it subject to warping if it is not braced.

Surface preparation is important with wood. Make sure the parts are clean, with no sawdust, fuzz, or stray wood fibers remaining from sanding or cutting. Go over the surface with a stiff brush to clean stray material, then wipe with a clean, lint-free cloth. Make sure that walls are braced sufficiently to prevent warping, as Chapter 2 explained.

Seal the surface with a coat of primer. This will give the finish color a uniform, flat base and will keep the wood grain from showing through the finish color.

I use regular interior or exterior acrylic house paint primer (fig. 21), but I put some into a one-ounce paint bottle (and label it) for convenience. Figure 22 shows the difference a coat of primer makes. Note how the wood grain shows through on the unprimed side, and how the paint is darker on that side.

Apply the primer with a flat brush (as wide as is practical), as fig. 23 shows, brushing the paint in the direction of the grain. Once the primer dries, examine the surface for imperfections. You can sand the primer if necessary and touch up resulting bare spots with more primer.

Add the finish color with a brush, airbrush, or spray can as with any other type of structure. The finished result, using a final coat of Polly Scale depot buff, is shown in fig. 24.

To keep walls from warping and to seal them so they'll be more resistant to changes in humidity, paint the back sides with a coat of primer (fig. 25).

## Staining wood

Sometimes a weathered, raw wood appearance is desired instead of a painted finish. In this case, stain and color the wood *before* assembly. If you wait to do this after a building is assembled, any glue seeping out of joints will prevent the stain from coloring the

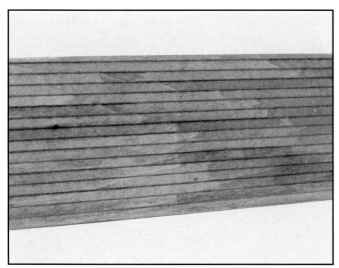

**30** The finished wall looks like it has been exposed to the elements for a while.

**31** Use a fine brush to apply rubber cement wherever you want the paint to peel.

**32** Rub the wall with a pencil eraser to remove the cement and expose the wood.

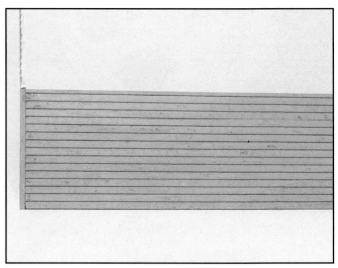

**33** The finished wall looks like it needs a fresh paint job.

wood. Seal the interior sides of walls with a coat of primer before applying stain or washes to the exterior.

You can make your own weathering stains by using artist's tube acrylic paints (see fig. 26). A small tin palette (found in craft stores) is handy for mixing small amounts. The best colors for creating weathered wood effects are black, burnt umber, burnt sienna, and raw sienna.

Squeeze a bit of paint into a cup in the palette as in fig. 26. Add water to the cup, then stir it with a small stick (see fig. 27). Don't mix the paint too thoroughly—you want to be able to vary the effect by how deeply you dip your brush into the mix.

Use a brush to apply the mix to the

wood, as fig. 28 shows. You can get varied effects by using multiple colors or by using thinner or thicker mixes of the homemade stains. Let the initial coat dry, and then highlight individual boards or areas with darker colors (fig. 29). Figure 30 shows the finished wall.

You can also get good results from commercial stains such as Minwax (found in hardware and paint stores). These come in a tremendous variety of colors and are easily absorbed by the types of wood used in modeling.

Let your walls and parts dry thoroughly (overnight at least) before adding glue and assembling them.

The photos illustrate a strength and weakness of wood. Weathering effects

vary because of the wood grain, but because the grain in sheet material crosses the entire sheet, it's often difficult to vary the effects much from board to board—the grain pattern often shows through. You have to decide whether the effect is good enough for your project. An alternative is to build up siding board-by-board as in real life. If you do this, be sure to stain all of the wood strips before beginning assembly.

### Peeling paint effect

We've all seen wood structures in real life where the paint is peeling—in some cases a patch or two here or there; in other cases, it's coming off in large pieces all over the wall. This effect can

# PAINTING PLASTER

Some craftsman-type structure kits have molded plaster walls, and you'll often find detail items molded in plaster. Painting plaster is not difficult. Most techniques for plastic and wood can also be used on plaster.

The main concern here is that plaster is very porous; it will soak up paint like a sponge. You can limit this by using an airbrush or spray can to give plaster surfaces a coat of primer or clear flat finish – whichever you use, make sure the finish is matte, not glossy. This will seal the plaster and make it much easier to get a uniform color with the finish coat.

Plaster can be airbrushed, brush-painted, or painted from a spray can. Brushes also work well for applying weathering washes to make the surface look more realistic.

Molded plaster walls are easily brush-painted because the surface won't show brush marks.

Weathering washes are also easily applied with a brush to subtly accent the surface of the wall.

be simulated using rubber cement.

Start by staining the walls the color of weathered wood as in the previous steps. Let the stain dry thoroughly. Next, use a fine brush to apply rubber cement to patches on the wall as in fig. 31. The rubber cement will act as a mask when the building is painted, so

apply the rubber cement wherever you want the paint to be peeling. For the best effects, don't apply the rubber cement in large patches. Keep each dab of cement on an individual board of the siding.

Paint the structure its final color. As soon as the paint is dry, rub an eraser

across the wall to remove the rubber cement (fig. 32). The cement will come off, revealing the weathered wood underneath. Figure 33 shows the results. You can make this effect as extreme as you desire.

**Good modeling paints include Scalecoat and Floquil spray paints, craft paints from Delta and other companies, and acrylic paint from Model Master (Testors), Polly Scale, and Badger Modelflex.**

There are many types of model paints on the market. I do virtually all of my model painting (both airbrushing and brush-painting) with acrylic paints. They are easy to clean up with water, and they work well on plastic, wood, and metal. Acrylics also don't have the hazardous fumes of solvent-based paints. My favorite brands are Polly Scale and Modelflex, both of which come in a variety of railroad-based colors as well as weathering colors (such as grimy black, roof brown, and rust), along with Model

Master Acryl. Craft paints are also good, especially for painting small details and figures. Delta Ceramcoat is a readily available brand.

Air is the main enemy of acrylic paints, so keep bottles closed whenever possible. If you're doing a lot of painting, transfer paint to a small cup or palette instead of keeping the bottle open.

Don't use spray paints or other solvent-based paints unless you can paint either outside or in a ventilated spray booth.

Simply opening a window for ventilation isn't enough. Wearing a cartridge-style respirator will also protect you while painting.

Flat finishes are needed for most model railroad work, including structures. Most paints designed for the model railroad market are flats, but double-check the label before making your purchase.

For an in-depth look at paints and painting techniques, see the book *Basic Painting and Weathering for Model Railroaders* (Kalmbach).

# PAINTBRUSHES

Paintbrushes the author finds useful include (from top) Kroeger No. 5/0 round sable, Model Master No. 0 round synthetic, Floquil No. 0 round sable, Model Master No. 2 round synthetic, Floquil ¼" flat Silver Fox synthetic, Floquil ¼" flat camel hair, Floquil ½" flat ox hair, Model Master ½" flat black sable, and Connoisseur ⅜" flat hog bristle.

You'll find several types of brushes useful when painting structures. The photo above shows several I use regularly. Large, flat brushes (¼", ½", and ¾") are good for painting large surfaces such as structure walls. Smaller brushes are sized by number: the larger the number, the bigger the brush. Number 0 and smaller (2/0, 3/0) are good for fine detail work.

Buy good quality brushes. With proper care they will last a long time and give much better results than dime-store 10-for-89-cents brushes.

Bristles are made from various materials. To get a smooth finish on a surface, it's hard to beat a good quality sable. Sable is soft and won't leave brush strokes behind, but it is also generally the most expensive type. I save these brushes for situations where a smooth finish is critical.

Synthetics will also provide a smooth finish and are ideal for use with acrylics. Smaller synthetics hold their points very well, making them ideal as detail brushes.

Camel hair is used in mid-quality brushes that are less expensive than synthetics or sables. They are fine for general uses, such as textured surfaces, where an ultra-smooth finish isn't needed.

Hog bristle brushes are quite stiff. These inexpensive brushes are ideal for dry-brushing, applying powdered artist's pastels for weathering, and applying a stippled finish.

It's important to keep your brushes clean. Wash them thoroughly after each use with a drop of liquid detergent and rinse them under running water. A rule of thumb is that when you're done cleaning a brush, you shouldn't be able to tell what color of paint you were using.

See *Basic Painting and Weathering for Model Railroaders* (Kalmbach) for more information on painting supplies and techniques.

A few simple interior and exterior details can make a model structure come alive, as on the loading dock of this modular HO scale industrial building from Design Preservation Models.

# Six

# Detailing

Assembling and painting a model gets you only halfway toward creating a realistic structure. Like an abandoned or vacant building in real life, even the most perfectly built model will look sterile and empty without details. We'll take a look at two basic types of structure detailing: exterior and interior.

External details and signs (we'll cover signs in depth in Chapter 7) are important because they're the first thing that a viewer notices, even from a distance. Interior details can be difficult to see, but without *something* visible through the windows, models will appear vacant and barren. This is especially true for storefront structures and other buildings with large windows.

Detailing can be generic—things that can be done to any structure—or specific to a certain kind of business. These details can help establish the purpose of a building.

## Interior detailing

Many companies offer interior detail items, including Evergreen Hill, Kibri, Preiser, Scale Structures Ltd., Walthers, and Woodland Scenics, to name just a few. Take a look through a large hobby shop, browse the pages of a Walthers catalog, or visit the websites of model companies (see Appendix on page 86 for a partial list) to get an idea of the items available. Figures 1 and 2 show just a sampling of the detail items available to the model railroader.

As with plastic kits, it's wise to paint details before using them, regardless of the color they're molded in. Remove flash or mold parting lines with a knife and needle file. Painting is a necessity with unpainted metal and resin

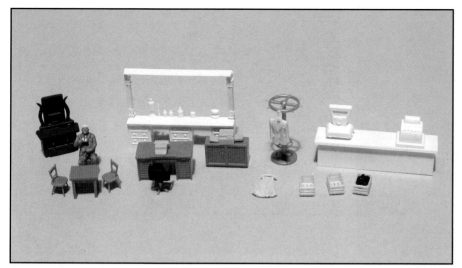

**1** Commercial interior details include tables, chairs, desks, clothing racks, and crates from Preiser. The furniture, store counters, and items are from Pola.

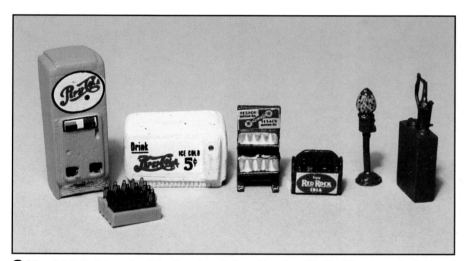

**2** Other details include cast-metal soda and gumball machines from Woodland Scenics, soda crates and bottles from Preiser, an oil can rack and soda six-pack holder from JL Innovative Design, and an oil rack from Great West Models.

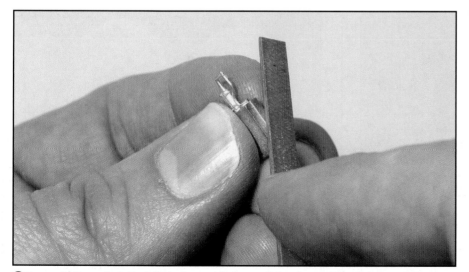

**3** Use needle files and a hobby knife to clean any flash or mold lines from metal parts before painting.

castings. Metal details often need more prep work than plastic items (fig. 3). Take your time and remove all flash, or it will be noticeable after painting.

Interior detailing doesn't have to be extensive to be effective. The lack of any interior detail is more noticeable than the presence of rudimentary detail. Since it's tough to get a good view through the small windows of models to see a dark interior, it's often sufficient just to create the impression that there's something inside.

## Window treatments

Windows are the first step in detailing. To create a lived-in look, almost every window should have some type of treatment. This doesn't have to mean a lot of work, however.

Smaller windows should receive blinds or shades. These are fairly easy to make and can be installed quickly. Figure 4 shows how they can be cut from file folders, construction paper, colored cardstock, or other paper. You can cut one piece of paper to cover many windows at once. Note how some give the appearance of closed blinds, while others are partially open. Vary the colors among structures (and even among different rooms in a single structure). Glue them in place from behind with clear parts cement, keeping the glue away from the window opening (fig. 5). In Figure 6, you can see the finished blinds.

Broken windows are a mess in real life but an interesting variation on a model. To model a broken window, cut a broken piece or two from a piece of clear styrene as fig. 7 shows. Use a scriber or the back of a knife blade to scratch cracks onto the styrene. The finished broken window is shown in fig. 8. You can use this technique occasionally on active structures, but if you want to accurately model an abandoned building, you should have broken glass in more window openings.

Another common real-life detail is the window-mounted air conditioner. Figure 9 shows a model casting from California Freight and Detail Co. (installed on a building from Design Preservation Models), but you could easily build your own from a small piece of styrene.

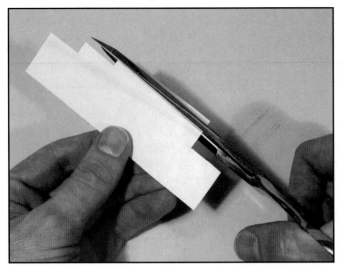

**4** Cut window shades and blinds from file folders or colored cardboard or paper.

**5** Glue the cardboard blinds into place behind the windows. Keep the glue away from the glazing in the window opening.

**6** The finished blinds give the building a lived-in look.

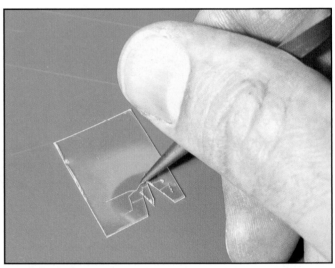

**7** Cut some jagged edges from a piece of clear plastic, then use a scriber to mark cracks in the surface.

**8** Broken windows add a touch of variety to a finished structure.

**9** Window air conditioners make structures look occupied.

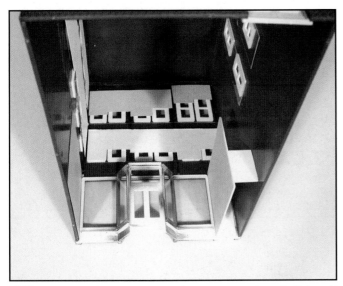

**10** Colored paper (with styrene backing) creates the interior walls that would be visible through the windows.

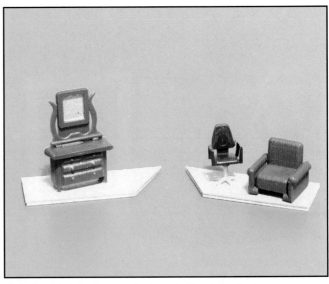

**11** Glue details in place atop the bases for the window displays.

**12** Glue the display bases in place behind the window wells.

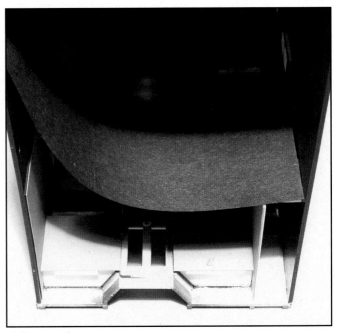

**13** Add a view block behind each window well. This one, made from construction paper, prevents viewers from seeing through the structure's other windows.

## Storefront windows and details

Because of their size, storefront display windows deserve special treatment. This takes more time, but it is worth the effort. Window display boxes are effective in storefront structures. When combined with a few well-placed signs, they give the appearance of interior detail even if most of the structure is empty.

Start by preparing the interior. Figure 10 shows an HO storefront building from Walthers that I decided to detail as a furniture store. I started by gluing colored cardboard along the interior walls, just to keep viewers from seeing red plastic walls.

Cut a piece of styrene to fit each window well. These will be the bases for the window displays. I used double-sided photo mounting paper (discussed in Chapter 7) to attach colored cardboard atop each piece, but you can paint them as well. Figure out what you want to show in each window, and glue the details in place (fig. 11). I used a chair and dresser from a Pola detail set (no. HO460) and a chair from Preiser.

Glue the window displays in place (fig. 12). I use clear parts cement because cyanoacrylate adhesive (CA) will fog the glazing and liquid plastic cement could seep onto the window. Once the glue had set in the display boxes, I added backing paper behind the window boxes (fig. 13). This effectively hides the blank interior, but to make sure viewers couldn't see through the structure, I added a view block of black construction paper (fig. 13). Figure 14 shows the completed

**14** It's obvious from the display windows that this furniture store is in business.

**15** Styrene shelves in the front windows of a grocery store holding vegetable crates are the store's only interior details.

**16** The vegetable crates on the shelves and the signs higher up on the windows neatly conceal the absence of interior detail beyond the window wells.

display window from the outside.

I recommend adding view blocks to any structure that doesn't have interior detail. This keeps viewers from looking, for example, into a second-story window and seeing out a first-story window on the other side of the building.

The furniture store was an example of a detailed window, but windows can be given more minimal treatment and still be effective. For a model of an old-fashioned grocery store, I built simple styrene shelves behind the front display windows

(fig. 15). I stacked rows of Preiser vegetable crates (some full, some empty) on the shelves to give the impression of a store showing off its wares (fig. 16).

I then glued several signs across the front windows as fig. 15 shows. Signs are colorful and add life to the structure. They also prevent viewers from seeing that the building's interior is empty. (Chapter 7 goes into more detail on making and using signs.)

The result is a structure that looks busy and occupied, even though the

interior detailing stops about a quarter of an inch into the building.

Use your imagination in detailing windows. You can fill a window box with tools and a wheelbarrow for a hardware store, or with scale figures to serve as mannequins for a clothing or variety store.

## More detailed interiors

Some structures, especially those with larger window areas, call for more interior detail. The Design Preservation

**17** This cafe has more extensive detailing, with tables, chairs, figures, a counter, and several signs.

**18** This City Classics gas station lent itself to interior details, including a figure, counter, signs, and window display including a tire.

Models HO scale cafe in fig. 17 is an example of a structure with a higher level of interior detail. Some structures have bases that serve as floors; for others, such as this building, it's necessary to cut sheet styrene to fit and glue it in place. (It's easiest if you do this work before adding the roof.)

You don't have to detail the entire interior. For the cafe, I added a floor and interior styrene walls to surround the dining area. Paint walls and floors (you can also cover them with colored paper or cardstock) before adding details.

The tables and chairs around the window areas are nicely detailed components from Preiser (no. 17201). The food, plates, bottles, and figures are also from Preiser.

The long counter is made from pieces of sheet styrene, with small pieces of styrene painted silver to represent napkin holders (once again, interior features—especially those set in from windows—don't require a high level of detail to be effective). The stools are simply small round pieces of plastic painted red and placed atop brass tubing.

A variety of signs on the interior walls add color and make the inside appear

busier and more cluttered than it actually is.

For the HO scale gas station from City Classics in fig. 18, I used styrene to build a small counter inside the office area, then added a cash register on top of it. The window shelves received typical gas-station items, such as tires.

A customer figure looking out the window and a variety of signs on the interior walls finished the office detailing.

## Loading platforms

Loading docks and platforms are among the best candidates for detailing, since they usually face the tracks and usually have loading docks for trucks nearby. Many companies make crates, boxes, and pallets (fig. 19), as well as barrels (fig. 20), garbage dumpsters (fig. 21), forklifts and carts (fig. 22), and other detail items appropriate for these areas.

Modeling a loading dock door open or partly open can add a great deal of interest to a scene. Figure 23 shows such a scene on an HO scale modular industrial building from Design Preservation Models. These are similar to the window boxes shown earlier, but on a larger scale.

You'll need to model the door or doors open or partly open. If the structure's door is thin enough, you might be able to cut it and reposition it. The DPM building had thick doors that would have been difficult to reposition, so I cut a pair of new doors from thin styrene (see Chapter 3 for details on how to do this) to match the kit's door style. After painting them to match the building's other doors, I glued them in place.

Another option is to replace the kit door with a simulated roll-up door. Most prototype warehouse and industrial buildings have roll-up doors for ease of use and increased floor space. An easy way to re-create this look is by using corrugated or V-groove sheet styrene glued in place behind the door opening, as fig. 24 shows. With this method you can model doors partially open or fully closed or open.

Use plain sheet styrene to build a box to fit behind the door. Paint the floor and walls appropriate colors (fig. 25). Glue various detail items in place,

**19** Loading dock details available include pallets from Pritchard (no. 5081), sacks (no. 17102), and boxes (no. 17100) from Preiser, and large cases from Kibri (no. 9458).

**20** Barrels include 55-gallon drums from JL Innovative Design (no. 313) and beer kegs, barrels, and milk cans from Preiser (no. 17105).

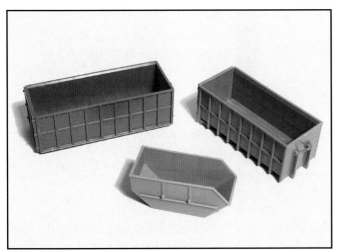

**21** Walthers makes a set of garbage dumpsters (no. 933-3516) that look at home near industrial buildings.

**22** Loading dock details include a forklift and fork cart from Kibri (no. 9458) and wheelbarrow and hand truck from Con-Cor (no. 9057).

**23** A few cases and barrels behind an open door add interest to a scene.

**24** Corrugated siding does a nice job of simulating a roll-up warehouse door.

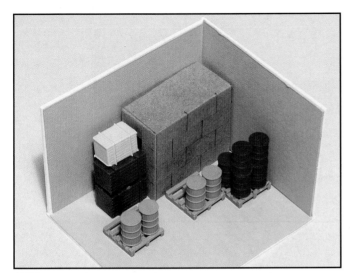

**25** Make a styrene box to fit behind the door. Paint the walls and floor and glue various details in place.

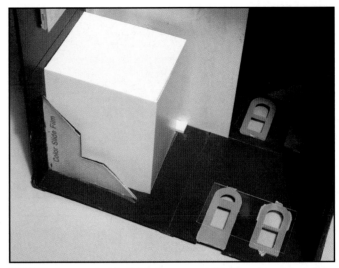

**26** This box was sized to fit into the corner of this HO scale modular building from Design Preservation Models.

keeping in mind the location of the door opening and likely viewing angles. Test-fit the box to the building and, when you're happy with the appearance, glue it in place (fig. 26).

Many kits of industrial buildings include loading docks and platforms, but you can make your own as well. I made a simulated concrete platform for the DPM building using sheet styrene (fig. 27). This is a small project that is a good way to get your feet wet scratch-building necessary detail items.

The platform itself is a simple box of .040" styrene. Platform height is dependent upon the door height. I cut the pieces to fit so the dock floor is even with the bottom of the doorway and it

fits between the end walls. The stairs at one end are made from short lengths of strip styrene (fig. 28). The dimensions can vary, but each riser should be a scale 9" or so.

Get rid of any joint lines between pieces by scraping along the joints with a knife edge as shown in fig. 29. Do this to the stairs as well to hide the seams between the styrene strips. This is an important step; doing it well will result in the seamless look of poured concrete. I finished the surface preparation by using a small piece of 220-grit sandpaper to sand all of the exposed surfaces. Sand in a circular motion.

I painted my dock with Polly Scale concrete. The photo on page 62 shows

the finished dock in place, with the figures and other detail items added. This type of scene can be the focal point of a layout.

Try to match the style of the details on loading docks and platforms to the style of the main structures. For example, a small building or business would likely produce a limited number of types and sizes of boxes, crates, or barrels, while a large company might have many sizes and types.

Also consider the era being modeled. Modern scenes should largely feature cardboard boxes on pallets, while wood packing crates and boxes were more typical through the early 1900s. Wood crates are still used, but generally for

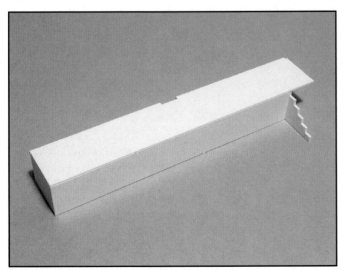

**27** Make a loading dock from pieces of .040" sheet styrene.

**28** The steps are short lengths of strip styrene, with L shapes forming each step.

**29** Get rid of the joint lines by scraping them with a hobby knife.

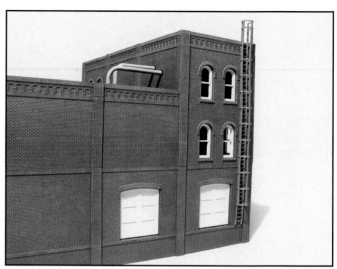

**30** Cage ladders (Walthers' HO scale no. 933-3515) are common on modern industrial buildings.

large or custom-built products. Large steel and plastic barrels are now commonly used for liquids, while wood barrels largely faded from use early in the 1900s.

The sidebar below shows an easy technique for making realistic cardboard boxes for a loading dock or warehouse.

### Other details

Keep your eyes open for other structure details. Fire escapes and cage ladders (fig. 30) are often found on city and industrial structures. Handrails and stairs are also common, as are wall- and roof-mounted fans, ventilators, and tanks (Chapter 4 shows many of these

roof details). Structure detailing is limited only by your imagination. Keep your eyes open as you travel, and study photos and buildings in real life to get ideas for your models.

Let's move on to signs—another great detail item that will finish your structures.

## CARDBOARD BOXES

Cardboard boxes are probably the most common way of packing modern products, but commercial models are few and far between. The photo above shows one method of making cardboard boxes using small lengths of wood, cut to the desired box size. Glue the wood piece to a plain

sheet of brown paper (such as from a grocery bag). Use a hobby knife to cut the paper to enable the ends to fold up and wrap around the sides, and the sides to then fold up and around to the top. Trim the top pieces so they match evenly. Use white glue to secure the paper at each step.

As an alternative you can create box art on a computer (or scan a photo of a box into a computer, then print it out) and wrap the artwork around a piece of wood.

This technique works well. Once you get the hang of it, you can make several boxes in a short time.

Hanging signs, storefront signs, and signs painted on buildings integrate structures in a layout and help define each building's purpose.

# Signs

Signs are among the most important details you can add to a structure. By using familiar names and logos, signs help make structures more realistic and place your layout in a specific time and location. This in turn helps viewers identify the theme and era of your model railroad. Signs make structures come to life, giving them a reason for being there.

Effective use of signs will also make your structures unique, helping them stand out from the thousands of otherwise identical structures on other layouts. You can customize structures with names. This allows you to re-create specific businesses along the railroad you're modeling. You can also immortalize friends and family members by giving them their own businesses.

A wealth of sign material is available, including commercial signs and decals as well as real-world materials that can be adapted to use on models. However, there are also ready made signs that aren't realistic and will detract from your structures and layout. Be picky, and don't be afraid to keep looking if you don't immediately find a sign that is right for a building.

Many structures come with their own paper or decal signs. Don't feel obligated to use them. The quality of signs included in structure kits ranges from decent to poor. Use your judgment, but remember that even the good ones are being used by many other modelers.

## Raw materials

Good-looking signs designed specifically for structures and scenery are available from many companies, including Bar Mills, Blair Line, and JL Innovative Design. Decal and dry-transfer signs are made by Microscale, Woodland Scenics, and others (fig. 1).

You can customize signs with decal or dry-transfer alphabet sets, available

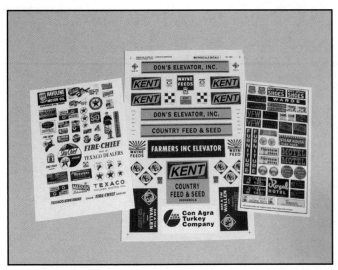

**1** Realistic signs include sign sheets from JL Innovative Design, decal sets from Microscale, and sign sheets from Blair Line.

**2** Alphabet sets are available in several styles and sizes, including dry transfers from Woodland Scenics, Clover House, and CDS, and decals from Microscale.

**3** Potential sign sources include road maps, matchbooks, credit cards, and stir sticks.

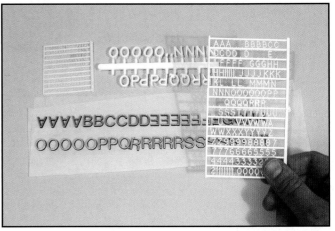

**4** Raised letters are available from Slater's; other styles can be found in office-supply stores.

from Clover House, Microscale, Woodland Scenics, and other companies (fig. 2). A wide range of lettering styles and colors is available.

If you look only at commercial products, you'll miss many of the sign materials available. You can find raw materials for signs wherever corporate logos are used, including road maps (oil company logos), stationery (look for notepads and other items used as give-away items), matchbook covers, business cards, envelopes, product labels, corporate calendars, novelty items, and magazine ads (fig. 3).

For three-dimensional lettering and signs, check out the line of injection-molded letters available from Slater's (fig. 4). These are available in sizes as small as 1.5mm up to ¼". For larger

signs, plastic letters designed for sign boards can be found in office supply stores. These also come in several sizes, ½" and ¾" being the most common.

Another great source of three-dimensional lettering and details is stir sticks (also called swizzle sticks), as fig. 3 shows. These novelty items can be found with raised letters in a variety of styles, all of which can be shaved off, rearranged, and used on structures (see fig. 5). The various shapes found on stir sticks (including cows, lobsters, chickens, drink glasses, hamburgers, and many other shapes) can be used either as part of a sign or on the structure itself.

You can often find the items mentioned above in antique stores. Although searching through these

shops can be fun, it's very much a hit-or-miss process, especially if you're looking for a specific logo. Tracking down these objects is easier now thanks to the Internet. The online auction service eBay is full of collectibles like stir sticks, maps, and promotional novelties. With the exception of a few highly collectible items, most of these things can be purchased for a dollar or two.

## Cameras and computers

Your camera also also be a great source of sign material. Almost any photograph can be turned into a sign, as illustrated in fig. 6. You can do this in a couple of ways: The traditional method is to take a photo with a conventional film camera, then have a

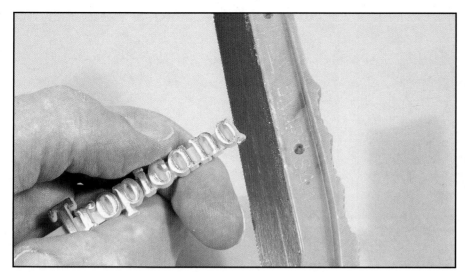

**5** Letters can be cut from stir sticks with a razor saw and used on structure signs.

**6** Photographs of real signs can be scanned into a computer, manipulated, and printed for use on models.

print made so that the sign is the appropriate size. Simply cut the sign from the photo and it's ready to use.

Digital cameras, scanners, home computers, and the availability of easy-to-use, inexpensive software for manipulating digital images have allowed modelers to create high-quality signs. Now, instead of simply printing out a sign, you can scan it into the computer (or take a digital photo to start with), correct its shape, color, or size, and then print it out.

Another option is to find logos on the Internet. Sources of these can include corporate home pages, sites selling products (such as eBay), or sites catering to collectors and history buffs

(excellent sources for logos from bygone days). Creating a sign is often a matter of downloading the image, sizing it, perhaps combining it with other elements, and printing it out.

Keep in mind that most of these logos are protected by trademark laws. For the most part you won't have problems if you download and print these for your own use, but you will be in violation if you sell or distribute the logos to others.

## Putting it all together

When you have all of the raw materials, you can start putting them together to create signs, including flat signs on buildings, hanging signs,

freestanding signs, and window signs.

The most important step in creating a realistic sign is to realize that few of us are graphic designers—we simply aren't qualified to design a realistic sign from scratch. If we attempt to do so, the results likely will be unrealistic.

Instead, take a look at real signs from the era you're trying to model. If you combine logos and lettering and copy the designs of real signs, you'll wind up with signs that look realistic because they're based on real ones.

Study the logos of companies for the era you're modeling, especially those found frequently on signs. These include beer and soft drink companies and chain stores. Many signs bore the company's logo, but with the name of a local business.

## Hanging signs

Among the most distinctive sign type through the 1960s was the hanging sign. These still can be found in small towns and areas off main thoroughfares. Figure 7 shows a collection of photos of hanging signs.

Making a hanging sign is a matter of securing your sign graphic to a piece of thick styrene and then mounting it on the structure. Start by cutting out the sign graphic, whether it is a printout from your computer or a commercial sign like the Blair Line product in fig. 8. Leave some material outside the final sign shape.

Cut a piece of .060"-thick styrene slightly larger than the sign graphic. Use a hobby knife to slightly round the edges of the styrene (fig. 9). If you want the edges of the plastic a color other than white—for example, to match the sign color—paint the plastic before assembly.

Don't use glue to secure the sign to the plastic. Instead, use double-sided photo mounting paper (fig. 10). I use a product, made by Model Builders Supply, called Stick'm that I found in a local hobby shop. Similar products are available at photography supply stores. Cut a piece of mounting paper slightly larger than the sign graphic and peel away one side of the backing paper. Stick the paper to the sign, then trim the backing paper to match the final size of the sign (fig. 11).

**7** Hanging signs are colorful and come in a variety of shapes and sizes. If you can photograph a sign, you can re-create it for use on a model.

**8** To make a hanging sign, cut out the graphic but leave some extra space around the edges.

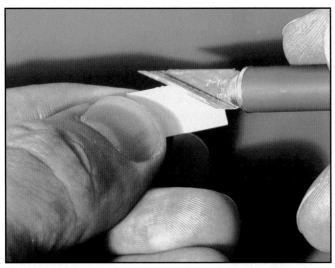

**9** Cut a piece of styrene to shape, then round the edges slightly by scraping with a hobby knife.

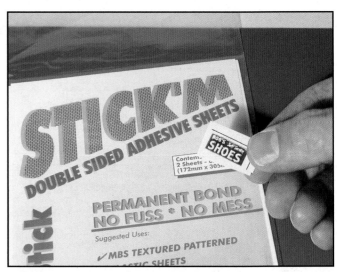

**10** Use double-sided adhesive mounting paper to stick the sign graphic to the plastic.

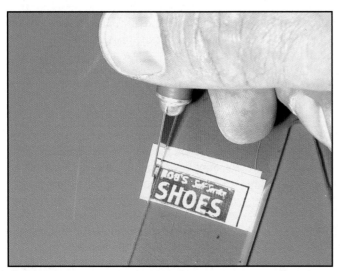

**11** Apply the backing paper to the sign, then trim it to its final size.

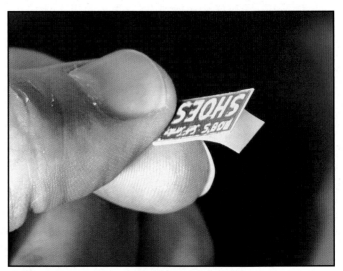

**12** Peel the backing paper from the back side of the sign.

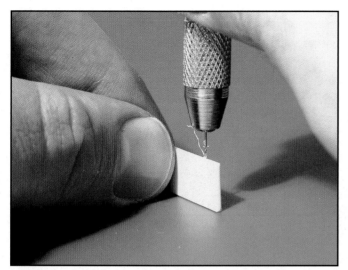

**13** Drill holes in the top of the plastic for the eye-bolt hangers.

**14** Slide a piece of mounting wire through the eye bolts and glue it in place with cyanoacrylate adhesive (CA).

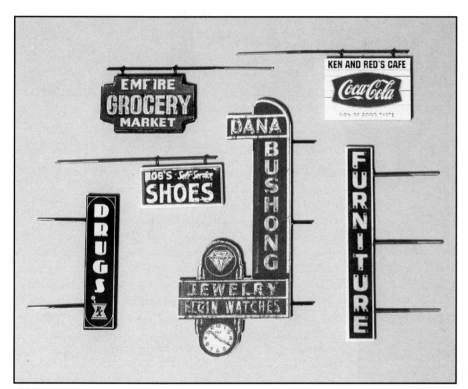

**15** The graphics for these signs came from a variety of sources.

Peel off the backing paper from the back half of the sign (fig. 12). Carefully align the graphic to the plastic and press it firmly in place. Using adhesive paper is a clean, neat process, much easier than glue. The adhesive grips instantly—no waiting for glue to dry—and the joint will last for the life of the model. There's no risk of glue seeping through and marring the sign graphic.

Repeat the process with the graphic for the other side of the sign.

Next, add a pair of eye bolts to the top of the sign (I used tiny bolts from Detail Associates). Drill no. 80 holes an equal distance in from each end of the sign as in fig. 13. Touch the stem of each eye bolt in a drop of cyanoacrylate adhesive (CA) and insert them in the holes.

Add the hanging rod through the holes in the eye bolts (fig. 14). I used Detail Associates .028" brass wire. Use a small drop of CA at each eye bolt to hold it in place. With a brush, carefully paint the rod and eye bolts a dark gray or grimy black color.

For vertical signs, drill two or three holes (depending on the sign's size) in the side of the sign. Slide lengths of .028" wire in each hole, glue them in, paint them black, and drill matching holes in the structure to hold them in place (fig. 15).

I prefer not to glue signs to my structures. This allows me to remove them for cleaning or for packing and moving the structures.

You can make signs as simple or as complex as you like, combining logos and alphabet sets. Complex designs can be made by cutting out multiple shapes from plastic. Figure 15 shows an unusually shaped jewelry store sign scanned from a book, a Coca-Cola restaurant sign with the logo taken from the Internet (and the lettering added via software), and several other hanging signs made from various sources. The photo on page 71 shows several types of finished signs mounted on buildings.

## Window signs

Signs and lettering painted on windows are common in real life. There are a couple of ways of simulating

**16** The drug store window signs were designed on a computer and printed out on clear acetate. The white lettering was painted from behind.

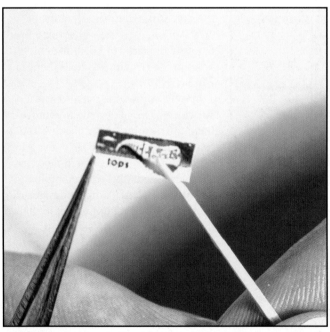

**17** When gluing signs inside windows, spread clear parts cement across the whole surface of the sign.

painted window signs on models.

The window signs in fig. 16 were produced the same way overhead transparencies are made. The text was created on a computer and printed on clear acetate using a laser printer.

Since this yields black graphics (although some color printers can also print on acetate), I printed the text in outline form, then used a fine-point brush to color in the lettering from behind. I used white, but any other light color could also be used.

Another way to do this is with decal or dry transfer lettering on clear styrene (*before* adding the glazing to the window). If you use decals or dry transfers, spray a coat of clear gloss over the lettering to seal it and hide film or transfer sheet residue.

Small signs in windows are also effective because they are visually interesting and can hide a lack of interior detail. They were—and still are—very popular in real life, especially in supermarkets, restaurants, and other stores. Glue them in place with clear parts cement, which dries clear and glossy. One trick in using these is to apply glue to the entire surface of the sign (fig. 17). This way when the glue dries it will be invisible. If you try to just use small dots of glue, they will show through the glazing. Several buildings shown throughout the book have this type of window sign.

## Painted-on signs

A common style of sign, especially in industrial areas, uses white block letters on a dark background. A prototype example is shown in fig. 18. This type of sign is fairly easy to reproduce in miniature, and you can make a genuine painted-on sign by using dry transfers as a mask for painting.

**18** Many brick buildings feature painted signs with white lettering on a black background. This one also has plenty of great details along the loading dock.

Start by figuring out how large you want the sign to be. Mask off the area and airbrush (or spray-paint) the entire sign panel on the building white (or whatever color you want the lettering to be). Burnish dry-transfer lettering in place on the white panel, using just enough pressure to transfer the letters.

Mask around the edges of the white panel so that the tape just covers the outer edges of white (this will give the sign a thin white border). Airbrush (or spray-paint) black in very light coats over the panel. Spray the panel from as straight an angle as possible so that paint doesn't creep under the dry-transfer letters. Once the paint is thoroughly dry, firmly press a piece of masking tape across the letters. Peel the tape back, and the dry transfer letters will come off as well, giving you painted white letters on a black background (fig. 19). Figure 20 shows the finished sign.

Here are a few things to keep in mind when using this technique:

• Use lettering styles appropriate to the era you're modeling. Compare prototype signs with available lettering styles. For example, don't use a 1980s font if your layout is set in the 1930s.

• Calculate the amount of space the lettering will take up before applying the dry transfers. You can use tracing paper to figure out how much space letters and lines will take up on the sign.

• If some paint bleeds under the

**19** Masking tape peels up the dry transfers that served as a mask, revealing the white paint below.

**20** The finished sign looks painted on—because it is.

dry-transfer letters, don't panic: Use a fine paintbrush to touch up any areas that need it.

Another way of creating true painted-on lettering and artwork is by making stencils. Use a computer to print out the lettering or artwork, then use a sharp knife to carefully cut out the letters (fig. 21). Tape the stencil in place, then lightly spray the lettering color. The result is a painted-on sign (fig. 22). This technique works best for larger, simpler lettering.

If the above techniques sound like too much work, you can simply apply decal or dry-transfer lettering as the sign itself.

## Billboards on buildings

Through the mid-1900s the large sides of buildings were looked upon as canvases for billboards and signs, as fig. 23 shows. Many of these can still be found, early 1900s advertising still visible in the twenty-first century. The structure sign in fig. 23 had been covered by another structure, preserved for many years, and then when that structure was torn down, the sign was again revealed.

Several techniques can be used for these signs. The easiest is to use decals, which will conform to the surface pattern (such as bricks or clapboard). Microscale has a number of decal sets, and several manufacturers have alphabet sets.

Follow standard decaling procedures: Start by applying a couple brushfuls of Micro Set to the building where you want the decal to go (fig. 24). After soaking the decal in distilled water, slide it from its backing paper into position (fig. 25). When that dries, add Micro Sol along the edges and across the surface of the decal (fig. 26). The Micro Sol will soften the decal, allowing it to conform to the texture of the walls (bricks in this case).

Once the decal dries, poke any air bubbles with a sharp hobby knife (fig. 27) and reapply Micro Sol (this process may have to be repeated several times). The finished decal will appear painted on (fig. 28), and it can be weathered to

**21** Lee Vande Visse made this stencil by printing out a sheet, then cutting out the letters with a hobby knife.

match the rest of the building.

You also can use the dry-transfer mask technique to create billboard-style signs on a building, as was done with the Berghoff Beer sign on page 71. The graphics for that sign came from a Clover House dry transfer set intended for use on a billboard refrigerator car.

You can make many types of custom signs by combining any of the techniques described above.

**22** Spraying paint through the stencil results in a painted-on sign.

**23** A razed neighboring building revealed this nicely preserved period billboard sign painted on a building.

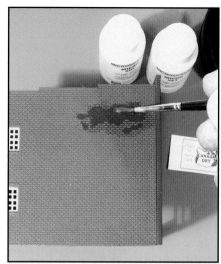

**24** Brush Micro Set where the decal will be placed.

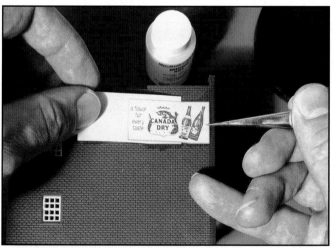

**25** Carefully slide the decal into place from its backing paper.

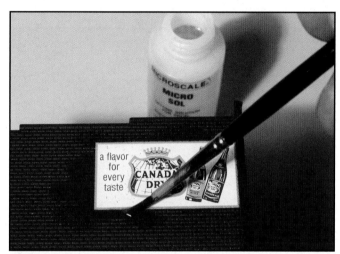

**26** Adding Micro Sol on and around the decal will soften it, making it conform to the brick surface.

**27** Slice any air bubbles with a sharp hobby knife and add more Micro Sol.

**28** The finished sign looks as if it was painted on the brick wall.

## Storefront signs

Most businesses are identified by large signs placed on the fronts of their buildings. These can be made using any of the materials discussed above. The horizontal sign over the window of the drug store on page 49 was easy to make. The signboard itself was included with the Bachmann kit. I painted it green, then added a 7-Up logo from a Microscale decal sheet and white dry-transfer lettering from Woodland Scenics.

Structures often lack these signboards, but they're easy to make. Start by cutting a piece of .020" styrene (.015" or .010" for N scale) to the desired size—usually the width of the storefront. The height can vary depending upon the style of the storefront and the placement of windows and other details. Make a border around the edge of the sign with .020" x .040" styrene strip (.010" x .020" in N), as fig. 29 shows. Paint the signboard the desired color.

You then can add lettering or logos of your choice to the board using decals, dry transfers, printed signs, or any combination.

The computer is an excellent tool for making storefront signs (fig. 30). You can use any drawing program (I used the basic AppleWorks program that came with my computer). Try various color combinations and lettering styles, then print them out (fig. 31). Use bright white paper for the best results; colored paper can also be used for different effects.

Add these to the signboard using double-sided mounting tape as with the hanging signs (fig. 10). Cut the sign to fit, then carefully attach it to the signboard (fig. 32). Glue the signboard to the structure, as in fig. 33.

Raised lettering gives structures a distinctive look, as the prototype photo in fig. 1 in Chapter 5 shows. You can use the three-dimensional letters shown in fig. 4 to give models a similar look, as with the Walthers HO gas station in fig. 34. Paint the letters before installing them (airbrushing or spray painting will give the best finish), and make sure the building is also painted before adding the letters.

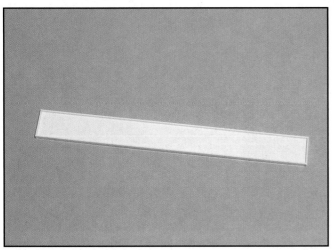

**29** You can make storefront sign boards by placing styrene strip around the edges of styrene sheet.

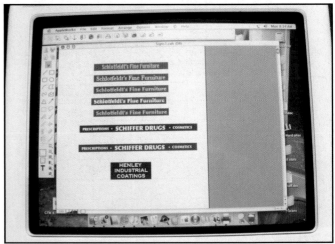

**30** Virtually any computer drawing software can be used to make signs in color.

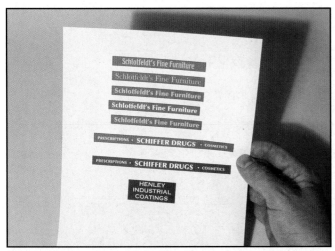

**31** Print signs and graphics onto bright white paper, or use colored paper for special effects.

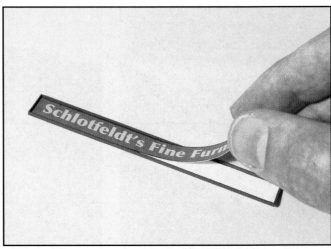

**32** Use double-sided mounting tape to adhere the sign to the sign board.

Place a small amount of CA on the back of each letter with a toothpick, then carefully set it in place with tweezers.

The free-standing gas station sign in fig. 34 was made by scanning a logo from an old credit card (fig. 3) into a computer and using photo software to alter the shape and flop the direction of the arrow before printing it out. The building lettering came with the kit, and the small signs came from a variety of sources.

Use your imagination when designing signs. By taking advantage of all the materials available, you'll be able to populate your layout with unique businesses that look as if they are earning their keep.

**33** The finished sign looks as if it was made just for this structure—which it was.

**34** The gas station's signs are a combination of commercial decals and raised-letter alphabets. The free-standing sign was made using a computer.

# Inspiration: Photo Gallery

**1** Above: You can take structure detailing to any level you desire, as Ron Morse has shown with this beautiful G scale store. Ron scratchbuilt the structure from stripwood and mat board, and he detailed the interior with scratchbuilt items, many of which he cast himself. He spent more than 1,000 hours working on the building. Ron Morse photo

**2** Left: Buzz Lenander combined tanks and components from a variety of sources to create an oil refinery on his N scale NTrak module. Buzz Lenander photo

**3** Jon Greggs built this impressive HO scale model of a steel grain elevator using sheet styrene and structural shapes, with details from a variety of sources. It was built to match a real grain elevator in Starland, Alberta, Canada. Jon Greggs photo

**4** Few home layouts can devote this much space to a scene, but it wasn't a problem for Chicago's Museum of Science and Industry. An HO layout at the museum features this Chicago scene that includes many high-rise buildings. William Zuback photo

**5** Large industrial buildings look good when they dwarf the trains, as with this N scale paper mill complex built by Bernard Kempinski. The tracks entering the building add visual interest, as do all of the rooftop details and the trucks at the loading dock. Bernard kitbashed a pair of Walthers kits to create the building. Bernard Kempinski photo

**6** Sheet styrene can be layered in complex patterns to produce many effects, as James Benini shows with this scratchbuilt HO scale art-deco car dealership. James Benini photo

**7** Interior lighting, combined with interior details, can add greatly to the mood of a scene. This is on Harold Dill's HO scale layout. Gary Hoover photo

**8** Building "flats"—shallow sections of structures consisting of a front wall and an inch or so of side walls placed against the backdrop—can be effective for creating the feel of a large city in a limited space. This scene is on the HO scale New England Rail, a club layout based on various New England railroads. Lou Sassi photo

**9** Above: Keep your structures in line with the era that you're modeling. Kenneth Ehlers has done that by using wood storefront buildings on his Colorado-themed Sn3 layout set in 1938. Kenneth Ehlers photo

**10** Having the trains run between structures can increase realism, as on this HO scale trolley layout built by Fred Miller. The tightly spaced structures and period details (the setting is the mid-1920s) make this a realistic scene. Paul Dolkos photo

**11** Effective weathering on this string of industrial buildings helps give John Wright's HO scale railroad a realistic feel. John models an industrial branchline on the south side of Pittsburgh in the late 1950s. Paul Dolkos photo

# LIST OF MANUFACTURERS

A.I.M. Products
P.O. Box 55
Schofield, WI 54476

AM Models (see Tomar Industries)

Alexander Scale Models (see Tomar Industries)

Alloy Forms (see Jaks Industries)

Alpine Division Scale Models
P.O. Box 6
Artesia, CA 90702-0006
www.alpinemodels.com

American Model Builders
1420 Hanley Industrial Ct.
St. Louis, MO 63144
www.laserkit.com

Atlas Model Railroad Co. Inc.
378 Florence Ave.
Hillside, NJ 07205
www.atlasrr.com

Atlas O LLC
378 Florence Ave.
Hillside, NJ 07205
www.atlasO.com

Bachmann Trains
1400 E. Erie Ave.
Philadelphia, PA 19124
www.bachmanntrains.com

Badger Air-Brush Co.
9128 Belmont Ave.
Franklin Park, IL 60131
www.badgerairbrush.com

Bar Mills Scale Model Works
P.O. Box 609
Bar Mills, ME 04004
www.barmillsmodels.com

Blair Line
P.O. Box 1136
Carthage, MO 64836
www.blairline.com

B.T.S.
P.O. Box 561
Seffner, FL 33583-0561
www.btsrr.com

Campbell Scale Models
P.O. Box 5307
Durango, CO 81301

C.C. Crow
P.O. Box 1427
Mukilteo, WA 98275
www.cccrow.com

Cibolo Crossing
P.O. Box 2640
Universal City, TX 78148

City Classics
P.O. Box 16502
Pittsburgh, PA 15242
www.cityclassics.fwc-host.com

Con-Cor
8101 E. Research Ct.
Tucson, AZ 85710
www.all-railroads.com

Creative Model Associates
P.O. Box 39
Plainview, NY 11803-0039
www.tichytraingroup.com

Design Preservation Models
100 N. Lake St., Box 66
Linn Creek, MO 65052-0066
www.dpmkits.com

Downtown Deco
5323 Fiddler Ct.
Florence, MT 59833
www.downtowndeco.com

Floquil (see Testor Corp.)

Gold Medal Models
1412 Fisherman Bay Rd.
Lopez, WA 98261
http://goldmm.com

Grandt Line Products
1040B Shary Ct.
Concord, CA 94518
www.grandtline.com

Great West Models
P.O. Box 224
Franktown, CO 80116

International Hobby Corp.
413 E. Allegheny Ave.
Philadelphia, PA 19134-2322
www.ihc-hobby.com

Jaks Industries
P.O. Box 654
Broomfield, CO 80038-0654
www.jaksind.com

JL Innovative Design Scale Models
P.O. Box 322
Sauk Rapids, MN 56379
www.jlinnovative.com

K&S Engineering
6917 W. 59th St.
Chicago, IL 60638
www.ksmetals.com

Kappler Mill & Lumber Co.
8908 108th St. N.E.
Arlington, WA 98223
www.kapplerusa.com

Life-Like Products LLC
1600 Union Ave.
Baltimore, MD 21211
www.lifelikeproducts.com

Master Creations (see B.T.S.)

Micro Engineering
1120 Eagle Rd.
Fenton, MO 63026

Microscale Industries
18435 Bandilier Circle
Fountain Valley, CA 92708
www.microscale.com

Midwest Products Co. Inc.
400 S. Indiana St.
P.O. Box 564
Hobart, IN 46342
www.midwestproducts.com

Miller Engineering
P.O. Box 282
New Canaan, CT 06840
www.microstru.com

Miniatronics Corp.
561-K Acorn St.
Deer Park, NY 11729
www.miniatronics.com

Model Expo
3850 N. 29th Terrace
Hollywood, FL 33020
www.modelexpo-online.com

Model Memories
P.O. Box 722
Powhatan, VA 23139
www.info-4u.com/modelmemories

Model Power
180 Smith St.
Farmingdale, NY 11735
www.modelpower.com

Model Railstuff
2686 Sharon Dr.
Adrian, MI 49221
www.modelrailstuff.com

Model Tech Studios
P.O. Box 1497
North Hampton, NH 03862
www.modeltechstudios.com

Modeler's Choice
1879 N. Neltnor Blvd., No. 320
West Chicago, IL 60185
www.modelerschoice.com

Monroe Models
P.O. Box 1120
Cokato, MN 55321
www.monroemodels.us

Mouse Models
P.O. Box 191591
Sacramento, CA 95819-7591

N Scale Architect
48 Kensington Ct.
Hackettstown, NJ 07840
www.the-N-arch.com

Northeastern Scale Lumber
99 Cross St.
Methuen, MA 01844
www.northeasternscalelumber.com

Northeastern Scale Models
3030 Thorntree Dr., No. 5
Chico, CA 95973
www.nesm.com

# LIST OF MANUFACTURERS

NorthWest Short Line
P.O. Box 423
Seattle, WA 98111
www.nwsl.com

NuComp Miniatures
P.O. Box 539
Bluffton, IN 46714
www.nucompinc.com

Pacer Technology
9420 Santa Anita Ave.
Rancho Cucamonga, CA 91730
www.pacertech.com

Period Miniatures (see Jaks Industries)

Pikestuff (see Rix Products)

Plastruct
1020 S. Wallace Pl.
City of Industry, CA 91748
www.plastruct.com

Polly Scale (see Testor Corp.)

Railway Models (distributor of Slater's alphabets)
P.O. Box 871
Edgewood, MD 21040

Rix Products
3747 Hogue Rd.
Evansville, IN 47712
www.rixproducts.com

Scale Structures Ltd. (see Jaks Industries)

Scalecoat Model Paint
P.O. Box 231
Northumberland, PA 17857
www.weavermodels.com

Sheepscot Scale Products
2 Country Charm Rd.
Cumberland, ME 04021
www.sheepscotscale.com

SignsGalore
109 Saligugi Way
Loudon, TN 37774-2518
www.tttrains.com/signsgalore

Slater's Alphabets (see Railway Models)

Smalltown USA (see Rix Products)

Smoky Mountain Model Building & Supply
P.O. Box 56
Somerville Borough, NJ 08876
www.drbens.com

Smoky Mountain Model Works
35 Springwood Dr.
Asheville, NC 28805-1626
http://smokymountainmodelworks.com

Special Shapes
1160 Naperville Dr.
P.O. Box 7487
Romeoville, IL 60446
www.specialshapes.com

Sylvan Scale Models
32229 Sylvan Rd., Rte. 2
Parkhill, Ontario N0M 2K0
www.isp.ca/sylvan

Testor Corp.
440 Blackhawk Park Ave.
Rockford, IL 61104
www.testors.com

Tichy Train Group
P.O. Box 39
Plainview, NY 11803-0039
http://tichytraingroup.com

Tomar Industries
9520 E. Napier Ave.
Benton Harbor, MI 49022
www.tomarindustries.com

Wm. K. Walthers Inc.
P. O. Box 3039
Milwaukee, WI 53201-3039
www.walthers.com

Woodland Scenics
101 E. Valley Dr.
Linn Creek, MO 65052
www.woodlandscenics.com

Yesteryear Creations
P.O. Box 2504
Florence, OR 97439
www.yesteryearcreations.com